Lowell Green

Here's proof
only we
conservatives
have our heads
screwed on
straight !!!

Spruce Ridge Publishing

ISBN 978-0-9813149-2-1
Printed and bound in Canada
© 2010 Lowell Green

This book was written, edited, designed, published and printed in Canada without the aid of government grants of any nature.

Library and Archives Canada Cataloguing in Publication

Green, Lowell, 1936-

Here's proof only we conservatives have our heads

screwed on straight / Lowell Green.

Includes index.

ISBN 978-0-9813149-2-1

1. Conservatism—Canada. 2. Liberalism—Canada.

3. Right and left (Political science)—Canada.

4. Canada—Politics and government. I. Title.

JC573.2.C3G74 2011 320.520971 C2011-906042-6

Dedicated to the memory of
Henry and Mabel Green, my grandparents,
whose generation made all this possible!

A proof is a proof! What kind of a proof?
It's a proof. A proof is a proof,
and when you have a good proof,
it's because it is proven!
— Jean Chrétien, cutting-
edge liberal thinker

However beautiful the strategy,
you should occasionally look at the results.
— Winston Churchill, cutting-
edge conservative thinker

Contents

Foreword

Forget the CBC's infamous "Vote Compass" online survey of political issues conducted during the 2011 spring election campaign. If you are unsure of your political leanings here is an easy way to place yourself on the political spectrum (at absolutely no taxpayer expense). Read the following quotes from British Prime Minister Margaret Thatcher. Then read the five statements that follow, identify which of the five you agree with, and you will have your answer. More importantly you will learn how many copies of *Here's Proof* you should buy!

Here, in part, is the statement the "Iron Lady" gave to *Woman's Own* magazine, September 1987:

> *I think we have gone through a period when too many children and people have been given to understand "I have a problem, it is the Government's job to cope with it!" or "I have a problem, I will go*

and get a grant to cope with it!" "I am homeless, the Government must house me!" and so they are casting their problems on society and who is society? There is no such thing! There are individual men and women and there are families and no government can do anything except through people and people look to themselves first. It is our duty to look after ourselves and then also to help look after our neighbour and life is a reciprocal business and people have got the entitlements too much in mind without the obligations, because there is no such thing as an entitlement unless someone has first met an obligation and it is, I think, one of the tragedies in which many of the benefits we give, which were meant to reassure people that if they were sick or ill there was a safety net and there was help, that many of the benefits which were meant to help people who were unfortunate—"It is all right. We joined together and we have these insurance schemes to look after it." That was the objective, but somehow there are some people who have been manipulating the system and so some of those help and benefits that were meant to say to people: "All right, if you cannot get a job, you shall have a basic standard of living!" but when people come and say: "But what is the point of working? I can get as much on the dole!" You say: "Look. It is not from the dole. It is your neighbour who is supplying it and if you can earn your own living then really you have a duty to do it and you will feel very much better!"

Here's how to grade yourself.

1. **Strongly agree**—you have the mature wisdom and common sense of a staunch conservative thinker and will need to buy

enough books to supply every neighbour who ever littered their lawn with a Liberal, Green Party or NDP sign. Enlightenment is your duty!

2. **Somewhat agree**—you are in the process of acquiring the full wisdom and elevated sense of understanding that every true conservative thinker possesses and will need to buy sufficient books for all members of your family to ensure you all progress up the ladder of enlightenment at the same rate.

3. **Somewhat disagree**—You fall under the "faint hope clause," and thus if you buy and read this book carefully, all may not be lost. You could very well be a late bloomer, so at least give yourself a chance at total enlightenment.

4. **Strongly disagree**—God help you because no one else can. Do not buy this book! It will give you nightmares!

5. **No opinion**—You are definitely an NDP supporter. Thinking requires energy that we all know creates greenhouse gasses and a terrible carbon footprint. By not buying this book you can save the lives of 2,312,000 trees! Or, if you want a peek at how we conservatives think, buy the eBook to keep your poor brain-washed conscience clear.

Chapter 1
Is Liberalism a Disease?

I only know him as Tom. Irish Tom, a delightfully opinionated regular caller to my Ottawa radio talk show who will launch himself into prolonged and furious broad brogue bombast at the mere drop of the words "British royalty" or "Liberal politician." Slipping those magic words into our conversation is a ploy I often use to liven things up on slow days. Tom never lets me down. He is an accomplished performer. Academy Award material indeed.

"Why are those bums coming to Canada?" He shouts into the phone. "Why are we even letting those parasites into the country?" (Referring, at the time, to the impending visit of Prince William and his wife, Kate, to Canada.) He winds himself into a full-blown Irish rage. His voice shoots up several octaves: "The Royal family—they're all bums—the most dysfunctional family in the western world—they should all be thrown out onto the street!"

At about this point I go for the *coup de grâce*. He pauses briefly for a breath and I manage to cut in. "And not only that, Tom, they're all liberals."

As always, he takes the bait, hook, line and sinker. "Liberals!" he screams. "Liberals! We should run the whole damn lot of those no-good bums out of the country on a rail." At this point my entire audience knows what's coming next. A punch line he's used dozens of times. He spits it out with glorious disdain: "Liberalism is a mental disease!"

I've done my job. "Thanks Tom," I say, "and next time…"

"Ya, ya." he says. "I know, I know, next time I call have an opinion; ya, ya." He chuckles and is gone.

Since most of my audience is Conservative or at least conservative-minded and thus has an advanced sense of humour I know all are by now bent over double with laughter.

Liberals not so much. The NDP and Liz May crowd not at all.

My experience is, the further left you are the less sense of humour you enjoy.

Socialists for the most part are a pretty grim lot and of course, these days you would be hard-pressed to find a Liberal doing a whole lot of smiling. Mind you, there aren't a whole lot of Liberals left to do anything! (I wonder if "Buffalo Bob" still thinks converting from NDP to Liberal was such a hot idea?)

Now I grant you, some of the "Dippers" seem like happy-go-lucky folks. Smiling all the time. I don't know about you, but the more they smile, the more they scare the bejabbers out of me.

With socialists, the broader the smile, the more dangerous the idea. Believe me, the lefties aren't smiling because they've got a great sense of humour. They're smiling because they've figured out how to save the world from big corporations/rich guys/global warming/little corporations/God/entrepreneurs/non-union businesses/oil companies/banks/George W. Bush/Stephen Harper/war/profits/famine/poverty/homelessness/disease/bad breath/warts/zits/ingrown toenails/pesticides/crime/guns/conservative broadcasters/private medical clinics/Alberta oil sands/massage parlours and—best of all—they've figured out how to GET YOU TO PAY FOR IT!

The NDP, very clearly, is Quebec's kind of party. Quebec, after all, originated the concept of having everyone else pay for what they want.

It's too bad most lefties have never given themselves the chance of hearing one of Irish Tom's famous rants because no one foolish enough to support the Liberals, the NDP or the Green Party would ever be caught dead listening to "The Lowell Green Show." At least they would never admit it. After all, most of what you hear on "The Lowell Green Show" is just common sense and what lefty has any interest in that for heaven's sake?

Here's another Lowell Green rule for you—the further left you are the more you claim you listen to and watch the CBC, when in fact you take great secret pleasure in either watching Charlie Sheen and Lindsay Lohan destroy themselves or catching Jersey Shore for pointers on how to improve the morals and language skills of your children!

Please note I've inserted a qualifier here in admitting that only most, not all, of what you hear on "The Lowell Green Show" is common sense. I confess that occasionally someone of a leftist persuasion bucks up their courage (or is heavily into the suds) and in hopes of embarrassing me, phones to challenge something I or a caller is saying. Common sense inevitably flees the airwaves at that point. Let's face it; common sense and liberalism/socialism are polar opposites.

Now I want to make this very clear, I am not suggesting that Irish Tom has it right and liberalism is a mental disease, but when you examine some of the things they advocate, some of the things the left has done, you really begin to wonder if maybe, just maybe, it's only conservative-minded people who have their heads screwed on straight!

I am a prime example!

When I fell under the spell of Trudeaumania in 1968 and tried to wrest the nomination away from a sitting Liberal MP did I have my head screwed on straight? Absolutely not. In fact as I look back on it now with a much wiser conservative mind, I have no choice but to conclude that I was a crazy man back then. Not only did I actually think I could defeat a well-established sitting member of Parliament, but this member—Tommy Lefebvre—was a perfectly bilingual francophone while I was (and am) an Anglophone with only a smattering of French. And this, for heaven's sake, is the Quebec riding of Pontiac just northwest of Hull. To make matters worse, I surround myself with other Liberals who are as deluded as I.

Obviously none of us had our heads screwed on straight!

Is it possible this Liberal nutbarism is bred in the bone? My father once ran as a Liberal in a southwestern Ontario riding that has been Conservative since Sir John A., for crying out loud. And, not satisfied with getting his foolish rear end firmly booted, he then, in the next election, turns around and runs in the same riding for the NDP! Who would even suggest he had his head screwed on straight?

In later life my father, like his eldest son (me), began to smarten up, became much more practical and realistic, which is to say a lot wiser, and declined to run for any office for any party.

Before I smartened up, I succumbed to Liberal Party entreaties in 1983 and agreed to run as a Liberal in one of the most socialist ridings in all of Canada. Now I've got to ask the question again.

Did I have my head screwed on straight? And once again the answer is the same—no!

Fifteen years have passed since my great Quebec election disaster. I'm still a Liberal and still not thinking anywhere near straight. So I get the nomination this time and even though Jean Chrétien campaigns with me for a couple hours one day, I get wonderfully whomped in Ottawa Centre by the NDP candidate. Actually, come to think of it, my ignominious defeat may have been Chrétien's fault since we were storming a seniors' residence that day occupied almost entirely by French Canadian women who went gaga over the little guy from Shawinigan but had no interest in the big guy from Brantford.

It was at about that time that my allegiance to leftist thinking began to waver. I have David Peterson, the Ontario Liberal leader at the time, to thank. Because it was he who unwittingly revealed to me one of the main reasons for Liberal success in this country. "Lowell," he said one day when we were alone. "Promise them anything. We'll worry about it later!"

Sadly, I did make some promises during that campaign. Promises I knew very well I could not keep. I suspect voters, recognizing my insincerity, did the right thing—rejected me handily—a fate I most definitely deserved.

But it wasn't until October 27, 1995, that my brain, and thus my head, became firmly affixed in the correct position. In case you've forgotten, that's the date of "The Great Canadian Unity Rally" when more than 100,000 of us showed up in Montreal to tell Quebeckers we didn't want them to separate. The day, in fact, when ordinary Canadians spurned the advice of Liberal Prime Minister Jean Chrétien and saved Canada from plunging into the great black hole of the unknown called Quebec independence.

When I say we spurned the advice of our prime minister, I mean exactly that. I recall it well. Throughout the later part of 1994 and increasingly through the summer of 1995 the signs were growing stronger and stronger that the majority of Quebeckers were prepared to take that giant leap over the wall of common sense and reason and vote to leave Canada. Huge sums of money were transferred out of Quebec; the military was put on alert.

You know the story. As a special Thanksgiving treat, Lucien Bouchard, now missing a leg, scared the bejabbers out of federalists and announced he was heading the separatist side and it appeared almost inevitable that we were about to pull the shades down on the Canada we grew up in.

You will also remember that through it all—even after Bouchard joined the battle—Prime Minister Chrétien arrogantly told us he had everything under control. "Not to worry," he told us, "leave it to my government to deal with; you people should stay out of this." Or words to that effect.

As the drama played out, I recall becoming increasingly agitated in my role as host of one of the most listened to radio talk shows in Canada. Much of my family lived in Quebec; many of my friends were there. Some of the happiest times of my life were spent in the province. As angry as I often was at Quebec for its incessant demands upon Confederation and the manner in which many Anglos were essentially driven out, I realized that I was not ready to say goodbye to the province.

And there was something else. Two days after Bouchard's dramatic announcement, I get an early morning phone call that sends chills down my spine. "The Crees will fight you know. We'll never agree to leave Canada." The voice is that of Billy Diamond, Grand Chief of the Crees of Quebec from 1974 until 1984, one of the most respected and indeed revered figures throughout the Cree nation in northern Quebec.

I had met Billy briefly a few years earlier during some business negotiations in Montreal. He told me at that time he was aware of the role my father had played—teaching Mohawk children on the

Kahnawake Reservation south of Montreal—and Billy claimed he often listened to my show when visiting Ottawa.

Here he is years later, using me to fire a warning shot across separatist bows.

"I'll deny it's me who told you this." He's almost whispering. "But you'd better tell your friends up there in high places that the Crees will fight to the death to preserve our place in Canada." I forget exactly what he said next, something about the soldiers of the new republic getting cold feet while tramping through the bush and swamps of northern Quebec, with Indians taking potshots from behind every tree. I do remember his parting words: "Mr. Green, spread the word the Crees will fight and you know the Mohawks. Do you really think they'll be signing any treaties with Lucien Bouchard or Jacques Parizeau?"

There's a brief pause before he says, "I couldn't stop them even if I wanted to." I try to ask him a few questions but it's apparent he's finished except to say again. "Spread the word! The Crees will fight!"

Stories hinting about possible native Indian armed resistance to Quebec separation began cropping up in various newspapers at about that time, so I suspect that mine was not the only phone call Billy Diamond made that morning. I understood fully what he was doing. Adding a vein of very tough gristle to the menu of filet mignon and caviar the separatists were promising their supporters.

Bouchard was convincing many Quebeckers that separation would be an easy stroll along Ste-Catherine Street. Vote "Oui" on October 30 and presto, come the morning of October 31, Canada says a polite goodbye, there's dancing in the streets, long stemmed roses all round, lower taxes, a Caddy in every driveway and a Stanley Cup every year for *les Canadiens*. Or something just as wonderful. No problems. Everybody agrees, handshakes all around, and it's over. Or so the separatists claimed.

Billy Diamond was simply trying to add a spoonful of reality and more importantly, fear, into the equation.

I'm still unclear what effect, if any, the threats had on Quebec voters, but the thought of armed Indians, possibly joining forces with disaffected Anglos launching some sort of guerilla operation in the deep woods of northern Quebec certainly scared me.

I knew there was no way Quebec separation could be an amicable walk in the park.

Many Anglos in western Quebec, especially in the Pontiac, begin making veiled threats about a separation movement of their own. Similar rumblings erupt in the Eastern Townships. There are questions about the fate of Federal Government employees living in Quebec. And what about Federal buildings? Who would own them? What about the St. Lawrence Seaway, the military bases, the banking system? If separation doesn't actually break out into some kind of civil war, it is clear the squabbling will last for years and likely send the entire country into a deep financial crisis.

As the October 30th referendum looms ever closer, we are staring into an abyss of indeterminate depth and danger. Heaven only knows what will happen with a "Oui" vote. Adding to my concern and the growing frustration of many, the Liberal government, and in particular Chrétien, don't seem to have the foggiest idea what to do about it. They all seem to be in slow motion, swimming in a muddy pool of denial and confusion.

I share my concerns and fears with my audience and along with CFRA morning man Steve Madely we use all our powers of persuasion to urge everyone to flock to Montreal on October 27, for a giant rally three days prior to the referendum.

I know I speak for Steve when I say we are both proud that many thousands of our listeners were among the some 100,000 who crowded into Place du Canada in downtown Montreal.

That overwhelming show of affection and solidarity for our fellow Canadians in La Belle Province undoubtedly persuaded sufficient numbers of Quebeckers to switch their votes from "Oui" to "Non" to prevent the country from being torn apart. But just barely. Canada survived intact by a vote of only 50.6% to 49.4%. Heaven only knows what the country would be like today had we not ignored Jean Chrétien's instructions to leave things to him and instead flocked to Montreal for that rally.

There is no question it was the Unity Rally that saved the day. Tens of thousands of ordinary people who took it upon themselves to step in and save the country that Chrétien and his party seemed bound and determined to fumble away.

Chapter 2

I Finally Get My Head Screwed on Straight

The October 27 Canadian Unity Rally in Montreal is also the day I finally get my head screwed on straight.

It isn't a straw that finally pushes me off the Liberal train wreck but rather a phone call toward the end of my show that day. It's from a very concerned and angry man aboard a bus on its way to the rally. "You damn Liberals," he says, "this bloody mess is all your fault." I'm taken aback. "What do you mean our fault? You can hardly blame the separatist movement in Quebec on Liberals."

"Oh yes I can and I do," he responds bitterly. "Look, I'm no political expert or anything like that, just a working stiff trying to stay afloat like just about everybody else these days. All I know is that we keep electing Liberal prime ministers, usually Liberals from Quebec, because they tell us they are the only ones that can keep the country intact, but let's tell the truth here. All you Liberals have ever done is give more ammunition to the separatists. All you do is stir them up…screw it up…make things worse…cause even more trouble."

Passionate, well-spoken callers like this, no matter what their stance, are more than welcome on my show so I'm only too happy to let him continue, although what he's saying is making me feel very uneasy.

"Look at Trudeau." he says. "He's the guy that really started all of this when he repatriated the Constitution without Quebec's support in 1982. And now look what's happening. Ever since the day he and the Queen signed that damned thing on Parliament Hill the situation has gone from bad to worse. More and more trouble. Downhill all the way. We've jumped from only 40 per cent support for separation in the 1980 referendum to probably more than 50 per cent support this time and you damn Liberals have been in charge for most of that time."

I try to point out that Brian Mulroney, a Progressive Conservative, was in power when the Meech Lake accord failed in 1987, but he isn't buying any of that.

"All Mulroney was trying to do with Meech Lake and Charlottetown was fix the mess Trudeau made, but now look at the corner your great friend Jean Chrétien has painted us into. And don't forget this is the guy who told us regular people to butt out. 'We Liberals will take care of the situation,' he told us 'don't worry, the Liberals are in charge!' Ya, right. Great job Chrétien. Great job you Liberals!"

I try to offer a half-hearted defence but his signal is beginning to fade. It is his parting shot that readjusts that final screw in my head.

"Ya," he says. "It was mostly you Liberals who got us into this mess and as usual it's going to have to be mostly us conservatives to get us out of it."

He is right of course, and what's more, I know it!

Chapter 3

"Non" Wins, Barely.

Three days later (October 30, 1995) a small crowd of grim-faced, obviously very nervous people, begins to gather around my makeshift broadcast location assembled on Montreal's Ste-Catherine Street just across from *la Baie*. Amazingly, local radio and TV in Montreal are providing almost no daytime coverage of this, perhaps the most historic event in Canada's history, so those drawn to our location are hungry for any kind of information.

I'm broadcasting to 12 different radio stations spread across the country from Halifax to Vancouver, so in an effort to paint as vivid and accurate a picture as possible of how Montrealers are dealing with what could be their last day as Canadians, I'm doing live interviews on the street and on several occasions we manage to hook things up so those gathered around me can talk directly to listeners in places like Regina, Edmonton and Calgary.

For the most part the Montrealers we're talking with are staunch and very worried federalists and aren't afraid to say so. It quickly becomes obvious that many of those outside the province have never really considered the plight of federalists, especially Anglos, in an independent Quebec.

One very concerned caller from Edmonton points out that this lack of understanding between the two solitudes is another failure of Liberal policy. "Most of us in the West never think of the plight of federalists in Quebec, mainly because no one has ever told us they even exist. When most of us out here look at Quebec all we tend to see is a bunch of damn separatists who never seem happy about anything unless we're pumping money into their pockets hand over fist! Hells bells," he says, "if I'd known there were so many loyal Canadians in Quebec I'd have joined you at the big rally down there!" It's a sentiment shared by several western callers.

When I raise the possibility of armed resistance from native Indians or others a look of concern and sometimes fear leaps into the faces surrounding me.

At one point a lively debate breaks out on-air between a federalist and a separatist. The federalist claims the referendum is really nothing more than racism—the separatist, of course, denies it. It's a very heated exchange that, as much as anything we have heard from either camp, illustrates the deep mistrust and animosity between the two sides. (When I interview that same separatist the next day after the narrow federalist victory he breaks into tears.)

The one thing agreed on by almost everyone—on the phone from faraway places and here on windy Ste-Catherine Street—is that the Liberals, from Trudeau right through to Jean Chrétien have really screwed things up. I make no attempt to argue with them. How could I?

It is a caller from Calgary who sums it up best.

"No matter what happens with the vote today," he says bitterly, "after this bloody mess anyone who ever again votes Liberal just cannot have their head screwed on straight!"

Thus is born a new Conservative and eventually, the idea for a book!

Chapter 4

Left Wing Bafflegab!

One of the reasons the left wing has been so successful in pushing its agenda onto the long-suffering and totally unsuspecting public is because of the special language the "progressives" use. A kind of lefty code you might say. In fact the word progressive itself is a good example of a code word that has been expropriated by the left as a signal of self-righteous, smug, self-congratulation.

In particular, the left wing has been extremely successful at rescuing obscure words and phrases from the dustbin of the English language or creating brand new combinations of words and even inventing some of their own. Never has the use of words such as progressive, sustainability, ecosystem, landfills, diversity, footprint, composting, closure, healing, and so on, been as robust as since the left wing and their brothers in arms, the environmentalists, expropriated those words and many others for their propaganda purposes. Phrases such as retrofitting, greening buildings, community initiatives, flex housing, solid waste management, moving forward, endangered species, wetlands, ecosystems, green energy and green jobs suddenly sprang to prominence.

Of all the lefty code words, however, the one I enjoy the most is the word "transparency." You would be hard-pressed to get through a two minute interview with Bob Rae, Elizabeth May, Al Gore or David Suzuki without "transparency" being dragged out at least a dozen times. One of the worst accusations hurled constantly against that "dreaded concealer of a secret agenda, Stephen Harper," is that his government lacks transparency.

It is especially delightful to hear anyone with the CBC using the word since it is highly doubtful if there is a publicly funded organization anywhere in Canada that is less transparent!

I suspect that there is an inverse correlation between the use of the word and the degree of transparency of the individual or institution using it. The more you kick around the word transparency the less transparent you are. It's certainly true with the CBC, but while the "Mother Corp" may have perfected the technique of essentially telling the public they have no right to know how or where their money is being spent so buzz off, others on the left have developed a very clever device to hide the truth, utilizing their special "code words." It's called "bafflegab."

A typical example of bafflegab perfected is a response one of my listeners received when he asked a city councillor exactly what the Community Sustainability Department of the City of Ottawa does, the same questions I have asked repeatedly for months on my radio program.

We're spending millions of taxpayer's dollars on something called the Ottawa Community Sustainability Department. Don't laugh, you probably have one of these things in your town, too. So my questions are: Exactly what do we get for our money? What is the purpose of this department? How do their highly paid employees spend a typical day? Since most of the communities involved have been around for a hundred or more years, far longer than any city councillor, they appear very sustainable to me, so how do you propose to improve on that and why? And above all else, please define sustainability. Exactly what does it mean?

Since I could never drag explanations from anyone, from city councillor to street sweeper, I assumed that no one—even those employed in the Ottawa Community Sustainability Department—had the faintest idea what it is supposed to accomplish. In fact, on more than one occasion I got the distinct impression that most of those around City Hall didn't even know that such a thing as the Community Sustainability Department exists.

Now, this is probably not that unusual. Mystery departments that serve no useful purpose other than to provide well-paid jobs and marvelous benefits to people who otherwise would have to really work for a living, or even go back to school to learn something useful at a community college, have sprung up like mushrooms in the musty dark corridors of government bureaucracies all across the country.

Thus it came as a great surprise to me when a rookie city councillor was not only able to track down the Community Sustainability Department deep in the bowels of Ottawa City Hall, but was able to get them to become "transparent" enough to explain to us great unwashed exactly what wonderful things its hard-working employees and managers are doing to justify their salaries.

As God is my witness here for the first time, word for word, is the official full and transparent explanation of what the Ottawa Community Sustainability Department does. The following is part of an email sent by Ottawa City Councillor Stephen Blais to one of my listeners:

> *The Community Sustainability Department, which works directly with our Infrastructure Services Department, is made up of a number of branches that perform a wide range of roles and responsibilities that benefit the residents of Cumberland and Ottawa.*
>
> *The Environmental Sustainability Branch provides leadership and expertise in environmental policy research, data integration and performance measurement to aid in the implementation of policies, strategies and tools to achieve sustainable development from an environmental perspective—A Green and Environmentally Sensitive City.*
>
> *The Sustainability Planning and Development Branch leads the development and implementation of the National Capital Region*

Planning Initiative which addresses and responds to the ongoing planning and development challenges of the City of Ottawa. Their task includes providing leadership, advice, facilitation, coordination, and integrated planning expertise to the development of a long-term vision for the sustainable community including strategic, business and neighbourhood planning.

Finally; the Sustainability Practice and Neighbourhood Livability Branch works to ensure that the sustainability practices are implemented across departments and communities.

These practices include providing leadership, support and guidance on the identification and development, monitoring and reporting, and benchmarking of key indicators at the neighbourhood and community level and report on progress in achieving long term development strategies.

There you have it. Pure transparency. And no, I swear on a stack of Gore/Suzuki gospels, I did not make this up. Could anyone, after having read this, not fully understand exactly what the Community Sustainability Department does and the wonderful benefits it provides us taxpayers? Could anything be clearer?

One thing is for certain. We conservatives across the country understand the various explanations perfectly. In fact we can explain it all with just one word—BULLSHIT!

Fortunately it cannot baffle conservative brains!

Chapter 5

The Pipe Dream Summit

The official title is the Sustainability Summit, held June 11, 2010, at Ottawa City Hall. The participant feedback summary, entitled *What was said, Sustainability Summit, June 11, 2010, Choosing our Future*, says:

"Over 200 community leaders, members of the business community, NGOs, academics, youth and representatives from all levels of government participated in the one-day event.

The purpose of the summit was to create the opportunity for community leaders to exchange views and identify strategies that would make the region more livable, resilient and sustainable."

This whole livable, resilient and sustainable thing got off to a rousing start when keynote speaker, John Helliwell, Co-director of the Social Interactions, Identity and Well-Being program of the Canadian Institute for Advanced Research spoke on "happiness." (Something achieved, apparently by fastening cute little leaf-shaped notes to trees!)

Since I could not possibility dream this kind of stuff up, allow me to continue quoting from the participant feedback summary.

"Throughout the day, local artists celebrated our vibrant community. The artists included slam poets, performers from the Ottawa School of Dance, and a Zumba dancer. Participants were also encouraged to write their ideas on paper leaves and post them on trees in the meeting area. (I swear on a stack of Gore/Suzukis I am not making this up!) During the small group discussions, participants also wrote their ideas on paper tablecloths set out for this purpose." (No mention of plastic scissors here or crayons!)

So what kind of ideas did our little kindergarten class (masquerading as community leaders) write on those cute little cut out maple leaves and the brown paper tablecloths?

I know this will fill you with shock and awe, but according to the Zumba dancing fans at the Sustainability Summit all we have to do to guarantee Shangri-La is simply enforce every liberal/socialist wing nut pipe dream foisted on the suffering public since Karl Marx.

Here are just a few things we will look forward to when the Sustainability Summit nut job graduates take over. The comments in brackets are my translations.

- People need to get out of their cars!
  (Turning all streets into bike lanes should do it.)

- We've got to have sustainable employment that we really enjoy.
  (Happy, well paid government jobs for life.)

- People must be stopped from buying so many things.
  (That certainly worked well in the Soviet Union.)

- We must be happy.
  (Only a Liberal/NDP government can accomplish that.)

- Individual behaviour must be changed.
  (We've got to vote Liberal/NDP, bike to work, use the green
  bins and smile more. Less flatulence would be nice too.)

- We've got to do a better job educating our students about environmental issues.
  (Teach them to vote Liberal/NDP, save the polar bears, build
  windmills in our back yards, bike to work, join a union, demand free beer.)

- Suburbs are not sustainable in their current form.
  (Close down all fire stations in the burbs and allow fire to do
  the job. "Burn the Burbs" becomes the new motto!)

- Renovate existing housing and building stock.
  (Each home must be remodeled to accommodate at least one
  homeless person or serve as a "safe injection site.")

- Limit development outside the greenbelt.
  (See previous page, "Burn the Burbs.")

- Generate alternate energy closer to home.
  (Backyards must now accommodate at least one windmill;
  every roof must be covered with solar panels. Hamster wheels
  must be hooked into the electrical grid.)

- Make bike streets.
  (I have no idea what this means. Do you?)

- Reduce our meat dependence.
  (They were able to accomplish this in the Soviet Union, North
  Korea and Cuba; why not Canada? A waiter who informed me,
  "Cuban cows have lifestyle issues" dissuaded me from ordering
  a steak in Cuba a couple years ago!)

- Plant indigenous plants on front yards instead of lawns.
  (Thanks to the ban on spraying, this policy is already well un-
  derway. Thistles and dandelions are wonderfully indigenous.
  So are the grubs and the skunks that plow them up.)

- Reduce waste.
  (The increased taxes to support all of these hare-brained ideas
  will ensure that no one has any money left over to buy anything to waste. We'll be scraping the glue off our wallpaper for
  dinner.)

- Reduce parking areas.
  (Bikes don't take up nearly as much space as SUVs.)

- Restrict the air conditioning in buildings.
  (Roast in hell you damn conservatives!)

- Educate citizens to better understand planning jargon.
  (Huh?)

- Create municipal facilities where people can get together and cook.
  (I am not making this up, I swear. The return of potlatches.)

- Provide healthier ways of getting to work.
  (Free mittens and ear muffs for everyone biking to work at minus 30 degrees!)

- Support an aboriginal peace and healing centre on Victoria Island.
  (A great place for a smoke shack.)

And finally this one that tops them all.

- Population must be controlled to allow sustainability.
  (China's one-baby-per-couple policy works very well. Just ask any of the 30 million female-deprived males.)

All of this nonsense apparently is the best that 200 of our leaders could come up with. And you can be absolutely certain there was not a conservative in the bunch! Please note that at no point was there ever a mention of how we are supposed to pay for all of these wonderful ideas, nor do I see a suggestion of who exactly would be in charge of controlling the population, although you can be certain it wouldn't be you or me.

Two hundred of the finest brains the left can produce and they didn't come close to the one idea that every conservative knows would make our homes, our communities, our cities a heck of a lot more sustainable and our people really, really happy.

All together now, conservatives, tell these lefty fruitcake Zumba-dancing goofballs the answer to real sustainability and happiness:

Lower the damn taxes, you bozos!

Louder! I can't hear you!

Lower the damn taxes, you bozos!

That's better. Thank you. If I send this message out to you written on a cutout paper maple leaf, will you post it on a tree someplace?

Chapter 6

Of Plastic Bags and Polar Bears

G ot a call not long ago from a guy with a very interesting question. "I had to pay five cents for a plastic bag to carry my groceries home yesterday," he said, "I understand that, but can you explain why they charged me an extra cent for the HST? I thought this five-cent thing was a charity. First of all, one cent on a five cent purchase is a 20 per cent tax, and secondly, I didn't think charitable donations were subject to tax of any kind!"

Coming up with answers to those questions took me the better part of a week and countless calls to various accountants, Revenue Canada and the Ontario Ministry of Revenue.

I couldn't get anyone to provide a reasonable answer as to why stores are allowed to charge one cent HST on a five-cent item, which is, as my caller pointed out, 20 per cent. One woman at Revenue Canada had probably the best answer to that conundrum when she chuckled and pointed out that, "It's pretty hard to find two thirds of a penny these days!"

The broader question however: "If it's charity, why are we charged any HST?" is much more difficult to get clarified. What it seems to boil down to is that the five-cent charge for a plastic bag is not a charitable donation even though part or even all of the money goes to a registered charity. As an accountant pointed out, when you pay that five cents you are making a purchase—a plastic bag—and thus the HST applies. The money goes to the store, and must be declared to Revenue Canada as revenue. If the store then donates those five cents or any portion of it to a registered charity then it is the store that gets the credit for making a charitable donation. There is no law dictating that the money must go to charity. (Whew, I hope you understand all of this!)

But yes you are perfectly correct, when you insist that both the federal and provincial governments are making money off what (in some cases at least) is in effect a charitable donation. In other words folks, we've been bagged!

The real scandal here is the fistful of lies we're being fed by various so-called environmental groups and individuals in order to justify the five-cent charge.

You may recall when these charges were first implemented we were expected to believe a fantastical story about a huge "island of plastic" somewhere in the Pacific Ocean. This island, we were told, is evidence of the terrible damage plastic is doing to the planet. We were absolutely assured that this five-cent charge will discourage people from using plastic bags, thus saving the planet from a horrible fate. Not only that but the money will go to help save polar bears, Blanding's turtles, spotted owls, wood chucking woodchucks, coyotes, and other assorted "endangered" species such as beaver and Canada geese.

At first we were told this island was twice the size of Texas. Then, before you could turn around, suddenly the "garbage island," as it is now called, becomes twice the size of the continental United States. And growing! Some reports claim the island threatens to engulf the entire planet!

Fortunately conservatives, with our superior intelligence, don't fall for this sort of nonsense, but the intellectually challenged "progressives" are thrown into such a tizzy that they ride off in all directions shouting, "Send money to Gore/Suzuki!"

To give you an idea of how crazy this whole thing is here are just a few paragraphs of a story written by Kathy Marks and Daniel Howden that appeared in an environmental publication called *The Independent*. This wonderful bit of fiction and many other stories that are even more like fairy tales appear widely today on the Internet and are read and apparently actually believed by tens of thousands of incredibly gullible people. (Conservatives, as you know, lack gullibility.)

Here's the story—as fanciful as anything the Brothers Grimm ever concocted:

A "plastic soup" of waste floating in the Pacific Ocean is growing at an alarming rate and now covers an area twice the size of the continental United States, scientists have said.

The vast expanse of debris—in effect the world's largest rubbish dump—is held in place by swirling underwater currents. This drifting "soup" stretches from about 500 nautical miles off the California coast, across the northern Pacific, past Hawaii and almost as far as Japan.

Charles Moore, an American oceanographer who discovered the "Great Pacific Garbage Patch" or "trash vortex" believes that about 100 million tons of flotsam is circulating in the region. Marcus Eriksen, a research director of the US-based Algalita Marine Research Foundation, which Mr. Moore founded, said yesterday:

"The original idea that people had was that it was an island of plastic garbage that you could almost walk on. It is not quite like that. It is almost like a plastic soup. It is endless for an area that is maybe twice the size of the continental United States."

The "soup" is actually two linked areas, either side of the islands of Hawaii, known as the Western and Eastern Pacific Garbage Patches. About one-fifth of the junk—which includes everything from footballs and kayaks to Lego blocks and carrier bags—is thrown off ships or oil platforms. The rest comes from land.

It is perhaps one of the most incredible stories of the past century and it all stems, not from reality, but from the very fertile brain of a guy who grew weary of his woodworking business in California and decided to go after the really big bucks.

His name is Charles J. Moore. He now calls himself Captain Moore and, as you can see from the *Independent* story, he is now being described as an oceanographer. He is no such thing. He's a woodworker who has a sailboat. At least he had a sailboat when he started all of this *Alice in Wonderland* stuff. He's probably got a lot more toys today.

Moore claims that in 1997 he took a shortcut in his sailboat from Hawaii to California and suddenly discovered what he then described as a "giant island of plastic" floating in the Pacific.

Astonishingly, during the several hundred years man has been sailing in those waters no one, until "Captain" Moore came along, ever spotted this huge island or took this mysterious "shortcut."

There have never been any pictures of this island and satellites can't find it, even though it is apparently twice the size of the United States. In fact, in 2010 a legitimate research team set out to find this mysterious island—they dragged the area with large mesh containers for an entire day and discovered less than a handful of debris further east—closer to the California coast. Where the plastic was supposed to be the thickest, they dragged their nets for an entire day and came up with absolutely nothing. Not a speck of anything other than beautiful sparkling clean Pacific water.

None of this has stopped Mr. Moore (sorry "Captain" Moore) from tapping into a wonderful money stream. To legitimize his operations, Moore founded what he calls the Algalita Marine Research Foundation and as a director of this very prestigious-sounding outfit he's written a few what he calls scientific papers setting off even more alarm bells about all the plastic that is supposed to be floating out there in the ocean.

Incredibly, many people actually take all of this nonsense seriously!

By the way, when Moore first declared he had discovered the "Great Pacific Garbage Patch" he claimed it was very visible. In fact let me quote directly from the biography of "Captain" Charles Moore that appeared on the Internet in February of 2010:

> *Oceanographic Research Vessel Alguita and its Captain found their true calling after a 1997 yacht race to Hawaii. On his return voyage, Captain Moore veered from the usual sea route and saw an ocean he had never known. "Every time I came on deck to survey the horizon, I saw a soap bottle, bottle cap or a shard of plastic waste bobbing by. Here I was in the middle of the ocean and there was nowhere I could go to avoid the plastic.*

This very visible island of bobbing plastic that stretched as far as the eye could see has now very mysteriously metamorphosed into a kind of plastic soup, which of course explains why no one has ever photographed it or seen it. It's apparently why satellites, which can find a tick on the back of a speeding camel, can't find it.

If you Google Captain Charles Moore or Algalita Marine Research Foundation you'll see even more fantastic stories about how this plastic island grows larger by the day.

You will also notice at the bottom of every website is a large billboard saying DONATE TODAY. CLICK HERE.

This wonderful fairy tale is one of the major reasons we are now dinged five cents each time we need a plastic bag to carry our groceries home, plus of course the one cent for the government.

The other reason for the charge is the poster animal for the World Wildlife Fund—polar bears!

Right from the start of this giant plastic bag rip-off we have been told by some retailers that proceeds from the sale of the bags were going to the World Wildlife Fund to save polar bears, which, according to the environmentalists, are threatened with extinction because of global warming. Sorry, climate change. (It's hard to stay current with the bafflegab.) How much money has been raised by all the stores charging for plastic bags I have no idea. I have tried for more than a year to get even a ballpark figure with absolutely no luck. Nor have I been able to determine how much money, if any, actually ends up in the pockets of the WWF that, by the way, has a truly incredible yearly income of more than 220 million dollars.

What I have learned however is that polar bears don't need the World Wildlife Fund, or anyone, to save them. Their populations in almost every area of the North are expanding so rapidly that hunting quotas are being increased almost every year. In 2011, for example, the Nunavut Wildlife Management Board almost doubled the number of polar bears hunters are allowed to kill in the Davis Straight area. This follows a 28 per cent increase in the quota allowed hunters granted for all of Nunavut in 2005.

According to the Committee on the Status of Endangered Wildlife in

Canada (COSEWIC) and Polar Bear International the polar bear population in the late 1950s had dropped to about five thousand. Today however these organizations report that there are between 22,000 and 27,000 polar bears in the world—about 15,000 of them in Canada. Furthermore all the evidence is that their populations continue to increase.

So much so that Simon Awa, then the Deputy Minister of the Environment for Nunavut, told me in 2006, "There are too many polar bears in Davis Straight for their own good."

Five years later, in May of 2011, I asked Mr. Awa, now retired from government, if he still shares the same view. "Absolutely," he replied. "My views today concerning polar bears are exactly the same as they were five years ago. Times are good for the polar bears of Davis Straight right now," says Awa. "It's thanks to an abundant supply of ring and harp seals. Seal hunting by humans has been greatly reduced and as a consequence we are seeing more seals now than we have seen for many years."

Mr. Awa goes on to say, "Polar bears have persisted through climate change cycles for millennia as have we the Inuit hunters. People all around the world are behaving hysterically. As a hunter, as an Inuk, I have first-hand knowledge. The idea that polar bears will be wiped out by global warming is just a scare tactic!"

Typical of the media treatment of the whole issue of polar bears is a story that appeared in the May 2011 edition of *Maclean's* magazine. Surprise, surprise, the story is topped by a sensational picture of a blood-covered, freshly skinned polar bear pelt featuring a bullet hole large enough to put your fist through. The caption beneath the picture says: "In search of big profits, hunters in Quebec are taking down polar bears at an unsustainable rate."

The story concerns rumours spreading throughout Nunavut that Quebec hunters had killed an inordinately large number of polar bears this past winter. The *Maclean's* story goes on to say that in fact many bears were killed, but for some reason the story fails to inform us exactly how many bears they are talking about. Nor is there any mention of the increased quota just granted hunters in Nunavut or the fact that the polar bear population is expanding so rapidly that in some areas they are becoming a dangerous nuisance.

What the story does is reinforce the totally false impression that not only are polar bear populations declining rapidly but that global warming is going to wipe the bears off the face of the planet.

It's another classic case of uninformed theory versus reality. The global warming theory from the professors, government experts and whacko environmentalists is that melting ice caps will deprive polar bears of food, thus virtually wiping them out. It's the perfect scare tactic that groups such as the World Wildlife Fund use to frighten the dollars out of the kind-hearted but gullible southern populations and of course persuade stores to ship them thousands of dollars from the sale of plastic bags.

The real experts however—the ones who live amongst the bears like Simon Awa and many others—say the theory about global warming killing off all the polar bears is just pure nonsense. The bears, thank you very much, are doing just fine they say; perhaps too well for their own good.

That's the reality but as we have seen time and time again when left wing theory comes up against reality the theory usually wins, no matter how wrong that theory may be.

And the conservative point of view on all of this? Easy. We made it very plain on May 2, 2011, what we think of left wing whackos and university professors!

Chapter 7

The Crow Solution

My grandfather, whom I believe did not know how to lie, told a story about crows which fascinates me to this day.

Curious about what he describes as "a huge racket" coming from a field at the rear of his farm one day he watched, through his binoculars, a strange ritual he always insisted was some kind of "crow court."

"There was a big circle of crows on the ground; probably a hundred or so of them making a terrific noise," he says. "All of them bobbing up and down very agitated and cawing like crazy. In the middle of the circle is this one crow, quiet, hardly moving. Suddenly, as though at some sort of signal, the whole circle pounces on the single crow and tears it apart. "It was really eerie," says my grandfather, "because when the attacking birds flew away they were absolutely silent. Not a sound came from them as they disappeared into the bush. I've never seen anything like it."

I have no idea if my grandfather was correct, but his theory was that the crow in the middle had done something that had endangered other crows, or perhaps resulted in the death of another crow. "One thing you've got to know about crows," he claimed, "is that when a whole group of them is feeding they always have a sentinel placed atop a high tree. At the first sign of danger the lookout alerts the whole crew and off they fly." His theory was that the crow was sentenced to death because it had failed in its duty to warn others of danger.

Are crows capable of this kind of group intelligence? I've had pet crows and can assure you they are among the smartest creatures God ever put on this earth. Certainly smart enough to stay far away from any place with lurking danger.

Which brings me to the situation we have in Ottawa where so many crows are assembling each night in the trees near the General Hospital that not only have they become a noisy, filthy nuisance they are now placing lives at risk.

Residents in the area complain they can't sleep at night with all the squawking and cawing; their lawns are a disgusting mess from the droppings. Even worse, crow numbers have now reached a point where they pose a threat to medivac helicopters that land in a nearby field when they fly in accident victims from throughout Eastern Ontario and Western Quebec.

"If something isn't done to get rid of the crows," say the pilots, "one of these days they're going to get caught in our rotors and we're going to have a disaster on our hands."

About now I can hear you saying, yes I can see it's a problem, but what have crows got to do with only conservatives having their heads screwed on straight?

Glad you asked, because this situation is as graphic an illustration of heads turned in the wrong direction as you will ever see.

Because in typical left wing fashion, a special city council committee has been struck to examine possible solutions. This has been getting worse now for several years so you can be sure we've spent many thousands of tax dollars studying the problem.

At one point, believe it or not, some giant brain came up with the idea of tying a live owl to a stake in the ground. They tied a string around one of the owl's legs; the other end to a stake driven into the ground, and sat back to watch what would happen. The theory was the owl would frighten off the crows.

Are you kidding? What happened was that the crows began dive-bombing the owl in huge flotillas. Wave after wave of crows would circle high overhead, give a powerful screech and plummet down to within a few feet of the poor cowering owl.

This prompted another marvelous brain wave. "When the crows dive for the owl," suggested one of the geniuses we employ at City Hall, "let's fire off some rockets or something to make loud booming noises. For sure that will frighten off the crows."

So just to add to the excitement, for a couple days, the neighbourhood sounded like the outbreak of another revolution in the Middle East. I told you crows are mighty smart, so it only took them the better part of one day to discover that the noise was actually kind of fun, a reward if you like, for their dive-bombing efforts. All noise and no pain! Really cool!

In all probability, similar attempts to get the crows to move on are still underway with the same results. Which is to say, each night more and more crows assemble in those trees. Some claim the cawing is sounding more and more like laughter. The cost, just like the droppings, continues to pile up.

In a letter to the *Ottawa Citizen*, Douglas Heyland, Executive Director, Science Institute of the Northwest Territories (ret.) claims that finding a long-term solution to the problem will be very difficult.

All of this a very graphic illustration of highly educated heads just not screwed on straight because, in fact, getting rid of the crows is amazingly simple.

Here's what any common-sense-blessed conservative would do.

Fire both barrels of a 12-gauge shotgun up into one of the trees one night. Bring a dozen or so crows tumbling down and you can be certain you will never see any of them again anywhere near that location. Crows are far too smart to return to any place where real danger exists.

Problem solved! One night. One guy. One shotgun. Two 12-gauge shells and it's all over but the final cleanup. My listeners, I am certain, would be only too happy to chip in for the cost of the shells!

In fact, I know several conservatives who would be glad to do the job at no cost to the taxpayer whatsoever. Heck, someone loan me a shotgun and I'll do the job myself. And yes, I promise to use only a gun fully licensed and approved by that other great Liberal problem solver—the Long Gun Registry!

Chapter 8

The Goose Solution

The caller to my show is almost crying. "I'm out here in my tractor planting corn, or at least I'm trying to," he shouts over the engine noise, "but the damn geese are snapping it up faster than I can put the seed into the ground. There's a flock of at least 100 Canada geese following me, gobbling up almost everything I'm planting and there's not a blessed thing I can do to stop it. If I shoot so much as one of the damn things they'll fine me more than a thousand dollars. What the hell am I supposed to do?"

He goes on to explain that he and several neighbouring farmers in the St. Lawrence Parks district of southeastern Ontario have tried everything to discourage the geese during planting season. They installed noisemakers, erected scarecrows, even tried some kind of special lighting system but nothing worked. The hundreds of thousands of Canada geese invading the area along the St. Lawrence River continued to not only destroy seedling corn and grain crops, but pollute the river and befoul the parklands as well.

Without realizing it, my farmer friend provided a graphic illustration of a very serious and rapidly growing problem plaguing dozens of countries. Canada geese are destroying crops, ruining grasslands, polluting parks, waterways and golf courses around the world. And it doesn't end there.

On more than one occasion flocks of Canada geese have brought down airplanes resulting in loss of human life. In 1995 a US Air Force E-3 Sentry aircraft, taking off from Elmendorf Air Force Base, Alaska, struck a flock of Canada geese with devastating results. The plane crashed, killing all 24 crew.

Immediately upon hitting a flock of Canada geese, US Airways Flight 1549 suffered a total power loss after takeoff from LaGuardia Airport on January 15, 2009. Veteran pilot Chesley "Sully" Sullenberger brought the plane down in what the media described as the "Miracle on the Hudson" in the Hudson River, saving the lives of all 155 aboard.

There have been many other incidents of aircraft crashes, along with countless close calls thanks to the burgeoning Canada goose population. Airports around the world are now spending tens of millions of dollars trying to discourage birds, primarily Canada geese, from congregating near runways.

What many don't know is that this is a fairly recent phenomenon. Canada geese were believed to have become extinct in the 1950s, until a small flock was discovered wintering near Rochester, Minnesota. Thanks to fines of well over a thousand dollars for anyone caught killing one of them, from that tiny flock has sprung what is rapidly becoming a worldwide scourge of well over a billion birds. Some estimates place the number at close to a billion and a half, with the population growing by tens of millions each year.

Here in Canada, killing a Canada goose is still considered a crime almost as serious as robbing a bank. But in New Zealand, where millions of the honkers have destroyed the pastures of so many sheep and cattle that farmers illegally shot and poisoned thousands in an attempt to save their fields and thus their livelihoods. The Government finally caved in, and early in 2011 declared open season on Canada geese. Today anyone in New Zealand can shoot as many Canada geese as they want.

In the United States some communities have begun programs of destroying goose eggs, and in some cases the geese themselves are being captured and destroyed.

Better yet, the US Department of Agriculture has launched a program of culling thousands of the birds, then donating the meat to various food banks. According to Hallie Zimmers of the USDA, each bird, on average, provides two pounds of meat; sufficient to feed three or four people. The meat is somewhat darker than chicken and is yummy good grilled, in casseroles or slow-cooked in crock-pots.

I can hear you asking again. Okay, so what has this got to do with conservatives having their heads screwed on straight?

The answer is pretty simple. Actually if your head is screwed on straight you already know the answer. If the Gore/Suzuki/PETA crowd would just stand aside and let conservative common sense take over, we'd turn farmers and hunters loose and allow them to shoot enough of the damn things (the geese I mean!) to bring their numbers under control and then turn the meat over to our food banks.

Knock off a million a year and we've got three to four million goose dinners every Christmas. The turkey growers will be mad as hell, but seriously, does it make any sense that while Canada geese are destroying millions of acres of food crops, polluting our parks and waterways and endangering aviation, our food banks are desperate for protein?

Actually, we'd probably have to shoot more than a million a year since indications are their numbers are increasing at a rate about double that in Canada. And while we're at it, instead of fining farmers $1,500 for shooting a goose that is destroying their livelihood, we should be fining the idiots who insist on feeding the birds during the winter, thus messing with their tiny birdbrains and persuading an increasing number of them to forego their yearly V-formation migration.

As usual the left has things totally backwards, which is pretty well the way their heads are screwed on. They think feeding the birds is being kind to them, when in fact what they are doing is messing with nature, creating a serious problem for the birds and for us humans.

Typical!

On the other hand, with a brilliant stroke of common sense we conservatives, with the aid of a few shotguns, would preserve precious food supplies around the world, make airplane travel safer, help clean up pollution from our parks and beaches, supply the poor and homeless with millions of pounds of tasty meat while providing some good healthy outdoor sport for thousands of hunters but Elizabeth May, Gore/Suzuki and their goose-addled leftist comrades won't allow it. Canada geese are sacred, they have decreed.

Believe it or not numerous of left wing lobby groups dedicated to preventing the killing of Canada geese have sprung up all over North America. Love Canada Geese, Coalition to Prevent Destruction of Canada Geese, Save the Canada Geese of Delafield, Wisconsin and The Canada Geese Citizen's Advisory Committee are some typical examples. Movie stars like Alec Baldwin have been recruited to the cause, so has the Sierra Club of New York and of course People for the Ethnic Treatment of Animals (PETA) is very much involved. There's even a special phone number listed for what is described as goose emergencies. Very clearly for those on the left, there is far more concern for Canada geese than there is for the hungry people they could feed.

Mighty strange isn't it? The self-appointed, self-righteous "progressives," whose constant mantra is how cruel and hard-hearted we conservatives are, when given a choice between geese and feeding the poor, choose the geese. Very clearly every conservative would choose to feed the poor. The idea of allowing millions of problematic geese to fly free while people go hungry simply doesn't make any sense to conservative thinkers.

Those who masquerade as environmentalists sign multi-billion dollar contracts for windmills which kill thousands of song birds, but defend the right of burgeoning and highly destructive populations of crows and geese to risk human lives, pollute our waterways and parks and destroy desperately needed food crops around the world.

So I ask you—who is the hard-hearted one in all of this? Who is the real environmentalist? Whose head is screwed on straight? What's very clear is that despite their claim to walk the high moral road, to be the friend of the "little guy," those on the left really aren't all that crazy about people of any size, although if you belong to a big powerful union the chances they'll like you improve considerably.

Very clearly however, there are a hell of a lot of socialists and even liberals who, when forced to make a choice, prefer crows and geese to people.

As they say, birds of a feather!

Chapter 9

The Tourist Attraction

Our tour bus pulls up in front of one of the most interesting buildings any of us has ever seen. "You may want to take a few pictures here," announces our guide. "This is one of Vienna's biggest tourist attractions."

"What a strange-looking beast, what the heck is it?" asks one of the passengers. "Believe it or not," smiles our guide, "it's Vienna's pride and joy—our garbage incinerator!"

Most of us aboard the bus can't believe it, but it is absolutely true. What we all gaze at with amazement, shaking our heads with a chuckle as we pop a few pictures for the folks back home, is in fact the Spittelau Waste Incineration Plant, located in downtown Vienna, listed by the United Nations as the world's most livable city.

This photo— a scan of a postcard bought in Vienna —will give you an idea of why it is so fascinating, so unique, that it has become a major tourist attraction in a city which itself is a huge tourist attraction.

This may be a bit technical and thus boring for some of you, but since most objections to high efficiency incineration come from the so-called environmentalists who like to throw around scary words, made up facts and junk science at us, I'm going to try to combat all that left wing garbage with some real facts and figures that come directly from the United Nations program called Habitat, and the City of Vienna.

Let me quote directly from information sent to me by the City of Vienna.

Methods

A storage depot receives deliveries from 250 waste vehicles daily, and holds reserves for three days. The trucks enter through an underground tunnel and thus do not disturb the neighbourhood. The plant itself comprises two boilers to produce steam from the waste. Attached to these is a counter-pressure turbine to generate electricity, four heat exchangers for district heating supply, and waste gas purification plants. To destroy pollutants in the boiler start-up and shutdown phases, a condition is imposed which requires the flue gas to be heated to a temperature of 850° C for at least two seconds.

The incineration process generates high-pressure steam, which drives a turbine and a coupled generator to cover its own electricity needs. If excess electricity is generated this is fed into the national grid, and during downtime for maintenance periods electricity can be drawn from the grid to power the plant. The steam and the return water from the district heating pipe-work are fed through a group of condensers. This enables the energy to be transferred from the steam back to water. Thus no water is wasted.

Experiences

The district heating plant at Spittelau generates 36,400 MWh of electricity in one year from 263,200 m^3 waste deliveries and heats 190,000 homes and 4,200 public buildings, including Vienna's largest hospital. Continuous checks and innovations in the waste gas purification plant are setting standards for the emission of pollutants.

Pollution Control

The flue gas is initially cleaned of solid particles by a three-stage electrostatic precipitator to remove dust. The gas then enters the first scrubber with water to remove HCl, HF residual dust, particle bound heavy metals, and gaseous heavy metals. The second scrubber removes sulfur dioxide. Then the gas is moved through a final electrostatic precipitator to remove the last amounts of dust down to a very small value.

Final DeNOx and Dioxin Destruction

The final treatment of the flue gas is in a DeNOx facility. The flue gas is subjected to selective catalytic reduction by mixing with vaporized water-ammonia and heated to 280°. **This results in the destruction of all dioxins.**

The flue gas is finally released to the 126-metre high stack. The emission of residual gases and solids are well below permissible amounts. An electronic billboard display outside of the plant gives the current emissions to the public.

Solids and Water Waste Treatment

All wastewater from the scrubbers is treated to remove the solids, that are formed into what is called filter cake. The resulting pure water is then released back into the Danube River.

All solids of slag, iron scrap and filter cake are further processed. The slag is mixed with cement and used for construction and iron scrap is recycled to make steel. The filter cake is bagged and sent to Germany as in-fill in an unused salt mine.

Conclusion

In the right environment, it is possible to operate a state-of-the-art *incinerator plant that disposes of solid waste, generates electricity and heat and meets very strict environmental standards.*

Canadian dump supporters please note, there is absolutely no odour of any kind emanating from the plant.

Those are the facts right from the horse's mouth, in this case the City of Vienna and the United Nations. In fact, talking about horses, the plant is only a few blocks from the home and training centre for the world-famous Lipizzaner Stallions.

Not only does the city boast that the garbage burned in Spittelau heats 190,000 homes and 4,200 businesses, but it has become a world famous tourist attraction.

Please note, this plant is not located in some remote location, but rather very close to the heart of one of the most beautiful and historic cities in the world.

The area is described by the City of Vienna as a mixed-use neighbourhood. That means it's right in the centre of an area featuring homes, apartments, and some commercial enterprises. A leading restaurant is nearby.

The Spittelau Waste Incinerator is, of course, only one of hundreds of similar plants scattered throughout most European and Asian countries. Interestingly enough, the Maishima Osaka Plant in Osaka, Japan, is almost a carbon copy of Spittelau and as a consequence it is usually one of the first destinations for Japanese tourists visiting Vienna. As one of our fellow Canadian travellers pointed out with a laugh, "the first place the Japanese want to take pictures of in Canada is the Anne of Green Gables House; in Vienna it's the place where they burn garbage!"

It is truly fascinating that throughout Europe the construction of high efficiency incinerators was largely due to the insistence of environmentalists. Sweden, the most socialist and environmentally conscious of all western nations, has been using incinerators to burn their garbage since the 1970s. In Stockholm you will find that the practice is so widespread that some of the larger structures have their own incinerator, which supplies heat and power for that building and sometimes several adjoining ones.

But here in Canada those who claim to be environmentalists have fought so hard against incineration that it's almost impossible to get a plant built.

The propaganda campaign against high efficiency incineration was first launched by then-Ontario NDP Premier Bob Rae (now interim leader of the Federal Liberal Party) who banned all incineration throughout the province. As a special socialist prize package, Ontario continues to be blessed with huge, polluting, unsightly, stinking, dangerous garbage dumps such as the one in Ottawa, which I have dubbed the Carp Mountain.

In Toronto when they ran out of dump space, they began trucking their garbage all the way to Michigan. Somehow the whacko left wing Bob Rae, David Suzuki, David Miller front-row parishioners convinced us that between 140 and 180 eighteen-wheelers whipping up and down the highway to Michigan each day was better for the environment than modern incineration.

Typical of the objection from so-called environmentalists was a phone call to my show on February 22, 2006, during the controversy that sprang up around plans to triple the size of the Carp Mountain. At the other end of the line was Rod Muir whose title at that time was Waste Diversion Campaigner for the Sierra Club of Canada. His call absolutely boggled the minds of more than a few of us when he claimed that as far as his organization was concerned incineration, even high efficiency incineration, was just as bad as piling garbage into giant heaps in the centre of our cities.

As further evidence of exactly who is stopping incineration, consider this quote from an article that ran in *The New York Times* in April 2010. The article was entitled "Europe Finds Clean Energy in Trash, but U.S. Lags" by Elisabeth Rosenthal.

> *Yet powerful environmental groups have fought the concept passionately. "Incinerators are really the devil," said Laura Haight, a senior environmental associate with the New York Public Interest Research Group.*

> *"Investing in garbage as a green resource is simply perverse when governments should be mandating recycling," she said. "Once you build a waste-to-energy plant, you then have to feed it. Our priority is pushing for zero waste.*

During the battle to stop the expansion of the Carp Mountain and subsequent to that, not a single so-called environmentalist organization offered any kind of support for the hundreds of citizens opposed to expansion of the dumpsite. Similar situations have occurred in several other communities across Canada.

When a petition of more than 1,200 names of those opposed to the dump expansion was presented to Ottawa City Council, it contained not a single name of any known environmentalist or environmental organization. Not even the Ottawa River Keeper expressed support despite the fact that there can be no doubt that pollutants from the Carp Mountain sooner or later end up in the Ottawa River.

And if you need further evidence of how out of touch with reality the Canadian left wing is consider this. The City of Ottawa, the Province of Ontario, Waste Management, and environmental organizations such as the Sierra Club all claim these huge dumps are perfectly safe.

"Don't worry about anything bad leaking out of these dumps and getting into the ground water or nearby waterways. Dangerous chemicals; terrible smells? Bah humbug," they say. "Don't worry, be happy, dumps are wonderful things," they assure us.

Then one day in the midst of all this controversy, lo and behold, former NDP MPP and extreme left wing Ottawa City Councilor Alex Cullen (defeated in the last election) issued a warning that we shouldn't throw any of these newfangled low-energy light bulbs into the garbage. "They contain mercury that might leak out of the dumpsites and create serious health problems!" was his claim.

Think about that please. The left wing won't allow modern forms of incineration that supply cities with heat and electricity and can even attract tourists. "The dumps are perfectly safe," they say "and are preferable to incineration." Then one of the left's top dogs opens his mouth to warn us that some of the stuff we put into the dumps can leak out and pose serious health risks!

The left's message then, as I understand it is as follows. The dumpsites are perfectly safe, but don't throw anything dangerous like a light bulb into them or they will become unsafe.

In short. According to Canada's "progressive" left, dumpsites are PERFECTLY SAFE. UNLESS THEY ARE NOT.

Preventing a Spittelau Waste Incineration Plant, or anything similar from being built in Canada doesn't sound to me like something people with their heads screwed on straight would do. But then let's not forget these are the same people who really believe that there's an island of plastic twice the size of the United States floating merrily around in the Pacific. Only good ol' "Captain" Moore has been able to find it. The "island" hides from satellites and other humans, but let's be honest here.

A huge floating plastic island is the left's kind of island!

Conservatives, on the other hand, prefer "The Island of Sanity!"

Chapter 10

Arlene

At least once a month I receive a piece of hate mail from someone who signs herself simply, as "Arlene." She isn't necessarily objecting to anything I have said, but what really gets her knickers in a knot is the fact that as far as she is concerned I take far too many vacations and obviously must have far more money than she has. The idea that any Canadian is successful enough to own anything more than a two-bedroom walk-up in a low-rent district seems to drive her nuts.

Her letters rage on about the injustice of it. What about the poor? Don't I care about the homeless? Her letters are filled with references to the rich getting richer while the poor get poorer with the obviously implication if we didn't have any rich people then we wouldn't have any poor.

Arlene makes no bones about the fact she believes I am one low-down, snake-bellied terrible excuse for a human being. Not because of what I say or do, but simply because I have been successful enough to be able to approach old age reasonably solvent. I suspect the thing she resents the most is the fact I have done this with absolutely no assistance from any level of government.

I take great pride, for example, in the fact that all of my books are edited, designed, formatted, published, printed, distributed and sold in Canada by Canadian companies with absolutely no grants of any kind from any level of government either to my publisher or to me. I suspect that fewer than five per cent of successful published Canadian authors can make the same boast. But then, you'll probably find that fewer than five per cent of books published in Canada by Canadian publishers have a conservative theme. And don't try to tell me it's because conservative writers are too dull and boring. Conservatives, no matter what they do are never dull and boring. Look at me for example!

Of course, none of this makes any difference to the Arlenes of the world, which makes her the poster person for something that has gone terribly wrong with the political left in North America.

Arlene typifies the left wing belief, prominent among socialists and other liberal thinkers, (some liberals are capable of thought) that success can only be achieved by the selfish and greedy through fraud or theft. As far as the left is concerned anyone who has been able to pull themselves up and out of the muck and mire of crippling taxes and government red tape to achieve any level of success must be an out-and-out crook. It is a misconception that is going to seriously damage this country if we can't shake it out of the general population.

Sadly the mainstream media have become the flag-bearers of this dreadful disease of cynicism about successful people.

What I would like to know is, where are the stories that tell the truth about how success is acquired in this country?

Where are the stories about successful entrepreneurs who, without benefit of silver spoon, government largesse or rich uncle, pulled themselves up by the bootstraps and built companies that employ dozens or even several thousand workers? These are also the people who help the homeless and the poor and the sick through their taxes and charitable donations.

Sure there are a few crooks out there like Bernie Madoff. There are always those who try to shortcut their way to success, but for every fraudster, crook and con man there are a thousand people like Al Saikali.

Chapter 11

From Worn-out Shoes to Riches

Let me tell you about Al Saikali, because his is a story that is repeated in various manifestations, countless times every day in this country. They are the heroes who keep our economy going. Sadly, his kind of success story is rarely told because success through blood, sweat and tears is something an increasing number of Canadians on the left of the political spectrum believe cannot happen without a whole lot of cheating, theft and various other forms of heinous skulduggery.

Al Saikali arrived in Canada from Lebanon more than 50 years ago. By his own admission he was very young, very naive and very poor. He literally owned nothing but the clothes on his back and one pair of worn-out shoes. As with most immigrants at that time, there was no welfare for him, no free accommodation, no English as a second language schooling. Only hard work and very low pay. It was, as my grandfather used to say, "Root hog or die!"

Al began his career in Canada by washing dishes in a bowling alley that has long since disappeared from downtown Ottawa. Sleeping on a distant relative's couch and existing on little more than crusts of bread and walking the streets to find whatever work he could, Al incredibly managed to save a few hundred dollars and went into business for himself.

As he explained to me, he found a tiny diner in what was then Eastview, a working class district in the east end of Ottawa inhabited mostly by recent immigrants and hard-working, blue-collar French Canadians. A small counter and a few stools were about all it could boast but the owner had a serious problem that was forcing him to sell at a distress price. Al walked in one day, shook out his pockets, plunked everything he had saved on the counter and told the owner he'd be back with a thousand dollars later in the day. The owner laughed but they shook hands, which in those days was all you needed to seal a deal.

Unaware that no one would loan anything to a threadbare kid with no collateral, Al walked into a nearby bank and demanded a loan of a thousand dollars. "What's it for?" asked the banker. Al told him. The rest of the story is hard to believe but Al swears up and down it is absolutely true.

"You want to buy that Eastview diner?" Al nodded. "He's got a serious problem there, you know that?" Al indicated he did and furthermore he knew how to take care of it. "Okay, you need the thousand dollars to buy the place. What about stock?" When Al tells me the rest he still laughs. "What do you mean stock?" said Al. The banker stared at him. "Stock—the hot dogs and hamburgers you are going to sell. You need at least another thousand dollars to buy stock, so I'm going to loan you two thousand dollars. Anyone who's been able to learn the language, work as hard as you and save the kind of money you have, will surely make a great success of it."

The problem, as Al explains it, was that the diner was being used as a kind of clubhouse night and day by a local motorcycle gang, whose members seldom, if ever, bothered to pay for what they ate. Al won't tell me exactly what happened, other than to say that he and a few of his Lebanese friends very quickly pitched in to clean up the diner, which consisted mainly of giving the motorcyclists the old "heave-ho" and convincing them never to return. Reading between the lines I suspect a few people got thumped!

And, just as that psychic banker predicted, Al Saikali did pay back his loan, and today, with two very successful Al's Steakhouses in Ottawa, I can guarantee you that because he worked night and day for more than 40 years, Al Saikali can afford as many cottages and beach houses as he wants.

How many people has he employed over the years? For sure many hundreds. How much money has he paid in taxes to help pay for the benefits never available to him? For sure millions! And is there any-one in this country who would deny Al Saikali his success? Yes, Ar-lene for one. Along with most of those who vote NDP, the Green Party and yes, I am sorry to say, many Liberals. Almost every single one of them believes the only thing Al Saikali should be rewarded with is higher taxes.

The left's philosophy seems to be, the more successful you have become, the more you should be punished with higher taxes, more regulations and more red tape and they're just the people who will gladly do it.

Among other things, the socialist crowd, of course, would do everything in its power to make sure your company becomes unionized to ensure that you are properly punished for having the gall to make a profit.

Incredibly, the left actually believes that the more money Al Saikali and anyone in private business makes, the poorer others are getting. Somehow they have come to believe that success and failure are some kind of balance scale. One guy gets rich, another one gets poor. The richer the guy gets, the poorer the other guy gets. It's a crazy idea, but talk to almost anyone on the left and when you manage to pin them down on the subject they'll agree that ya, that's pretty well the way it works.

Conservatives know all about starting with nothing, working hard and taking risks. That's why almost everyone who has done well, especially business people, are Conservatives. But make no mistake about this—success didn't turn them into Conservatives. It's the fact that they are conservative in nature that led to their success. This is not a "which came first the chicken or the egg" question. In almost every case, first came the conservatism then came the success.

If you're looking for proof that success is almost always the product of hard work and risk taking, consider a survey carried out in early 2011 by Harris Decima that showed that fully 94 per cent of Canadians with more than $1 million to invest are self-made. Only six per cent said they owe most of their wealth to inheritance. Andrew Auerbach, vice-president of BMO Private Banking in Toronto says if the survey were to look at what he calls "ultra-high net worth families," those with more than $10 million in investable assets, the slant towards the self-made would be even greater. Auerbach says the main point to be taken from the survey is that Canadians should feel good about living in a country where upward mobility is possible. "These findings speak to the strong entrepreneurial environment in which we live," he says.

And believe me, every conservative understands fully that the more money Al Saikali and others like him make, the more jobs they will create and the more people they will support with taxes and charity.

I doubt there is a true conservative anywhere in the country who would not be proud to shake Al Saikali's hand. Because they know if Al Saikali can make it here, so can they!

This terrible cynicism about individual, and in particular, entrepreneurial success is an integral part of the cultural civil war raging in our country. It is destructive. Not only to those who achieve some success, but to those who harbour contempt for the ethic of self-reliance.

This belief helps to create a culture of dependence. A belief that someone else—mostly big government—will look after you. As a consequence we have far too many people in this country who believe they have no responsibility for their own success or lack thereof. It's a cynicism that promotes the idea that the individual has no control over his or her own life; that you cannot steer your own course, that whatever happens to you has nothing to do with the choices you make.

Rush Limbaugh, the conservative talk show host who dominates American radio airwaves tells the story of the time immediately following the 1992 Rodney King riots in Los Angles when block after block of the city was reduced to smoldering rubble. "There," says Limbaugh, "were long lines of people forming in front of the piles of brick and glass shards where the U.S. Post Office had once stood. People were gathering as usual, lining up for their welfare cheques. As the camera pans the faces of the crowd many of the people have tears streaming down their cheeks. So dependent upon Government assistance are they that they are incapable of understanding that piles of rubble cannot help you."

What Rush doesn't say is that in some cases, those lining up for their welfare money had taken part in destroying the buildings from which the cheques had until now been issued. Such is the terrible power of dependency.

Conservatives understand this and fight continually for smaller government, lower taxes, more self-reliance, more individual responsibility and less dependency upon all forms of government. And, of this you can be certain, those with conservative convictions know very well that if the poor really do get poorer it's not because the rich are getting richer. Even Gore/Suzuki cannot make the poor get rich by making the rich poorer.

The poor can get rich by doing what the rich do. Doesn't that make sense?

As my father once told me, any damn fool knows the way to free a horse stuck in a ditch is to pull him out, not get down there stuck with him!

I don't know about you but I'm glad we live in a country where through hard work, making sacrifices and taking risks, guys like Al Saikali can get rich. Thank goodness it's happening all the time all around us although you seldom hear about it. The media used to be filled with success stories. Books were written and movies made about heroes who fought through adversity to achieve great success. Hard work was revered and honoured. No longer! An entire generation of children grew up reading Horatio Alger's series of books that pretty well defined the phrase "pulling yourself up by your bootstraps." Titles such as *Ragged Dick, Risen from the Ranks* and the *Luck and Pluck* series inspired legions of young people to seek a better life. Is there anything comparable today? I haven't seen it. Have you?

I recall back in the 70s interviewing Colonel Harland Sanders. His stories of going without sleep for days on end while driving thousands of miles in an effort to make a sale of his fried chicken still sends shivers up and down my spine. He boasted of going bankrupt 12 times before he finally hit it big. "If you haven't hit the canvas a few times in your life," he told me, "you just ain't trying hard enough!"

Today, of course, the media are much more interested in the great failures of our day. Page after page is devoted to spoiled, drunken and drugged up celebrities. Wall-to-wall coverage of Charlie Sheen, Paris Hilton and Lindsay Lohan and the latest inmate of the Betty Ford Clinic have supplanted stories about the folks like Colonel Sanders in our midst.

Don't get me wrong. The success stories are still out there. More than ever. There's probably one lurking just around your corner at the local Mac's Milk store. Sadly, success stories just aren't fashionable anymore. Certainly not in the left wing media.

I once responded to Arlene, suggesting that she should be rejoicing at the fact that I have been able to acquire at least a moderate amount of wealth. After all, if a Canadian can't afford some of the finer things in life after working non-stop for 55 years and counting, then there's not much hope for anyone is there? Certainly not for Arlene.

But that's the problem isn't it? Arlene, and far too many like her, don't believe they have achieved the success they fully deserve. And in keeping with left wing ideology, it's not their fault. They are firmly convinced that their unhappiness is society's fault, which really means it's entirely our fault—yours and mine. It's especially our fault if we are the least bit successful.

The Arlenes of the world honestly believe that the success of others is what robs them of theirs. This dangerous idea that success or failure is something that is done to you rather than something you do to yourself is fed to our children these days almost with their mother's milk.

Chapter 12

Pouring Milk on Your Kid's Corn Flakes

The great English essayist Samuel Johnson may or may not have coined the phrase the road to hell is paved with good intentions. Whoever did write it must have had our school breakfast clubs in mind. Because if ever there was a good intention paving the road to hell it must surely be those well-intentioned but terribly deluded souls who are replacing parents as breakfast providers each school morning.

The left has screwed up our thinking so badly that many people actually think absolving parents of the task of pouring milk over their child's cornflakes is doing the kid a great favour.

Breakfast is the most important meal of the day they say. Children are coming to school hungry; we've got to feed them. But wait just a minute here. Who's raising these kids anyway? The parents or the school? If breakfast is such an important meal why don't we insist that the parents provide it? And if for some reason the parents can't or won't feed their children the most important meal of the day, we had bloody well better find out what's going on in that household and get it fixed. That's what we would do if we really cared about the child.

Breakfast is the cheapest and easiest meal of the day to prepare. If there's no food in the house we had better make sure we find out why not and get some in there. If the parents won't get their sorry butts out of bed in the morning then we had better put the fear of the Children's Aid Society (CAS) or something into them. Failing to feed your child the most important meal of the day surely is child abuse. Treat it as such and for heaven's sake stop facilitating the parent's irresponsible behaviour. And please keep this in mind. If a child is not getting a proper breakfast on school days, chances are pretty good the same holds true during school holidays which these days is pretty well half the year. Once again, if we really were concerned about the child we would make sure he or she gets a proper breakfast each morning, not just when school is in session.

They figured this out a long time ago in the town of Laval, just north of Montreal. There, if a teacher suspects a child is not receiving a proper breakfast before coming to school, she notifies a team of volunteers who will check with the parents involved to see what the problem is. Very quietly, so that none of the other children get wind of it, they call on the child's home, first of all to inform the parents their children don't appear to be getting a proper breakfast and then inquiring if there is anything they can do to help. In other words if there really isn't sufficient food in the house they will make sure that from now on there is. Several local stores are ready to provide whatever is required free of charge.

Interestingly enough they found that in nearly 90 per cent of the cases, the parents didn't know there was any kind of problem. Or at least so they claimed. In many cases the parents left for work early and honestly thought their kids were preparing their own breakfast. In a few situations real neglect was observed and the situation was turned over to the CAS. There were a few instances of parents objecting to what they deemed to be do-gooders or busybodies snooping around, but in the end the problem of children showing up for class hungry ended, which, after all, should be the goal.

According to one volunteer I spoke with in Laval, the mere fact that everyone understands children are monitored and required to have a proper breakfast is sufficient to ensure parental responsibility. Amazing isn't it? Provide some consequences and problem solved. The civil libertarians of course would consider this an invasion of privacy and the child be damned. Well they wouldn't actually say child be damned but that would be the end result.

One other thing they do in Laval is actually show children how to prepare healthy meals on their own, including breakfast, during health classes. What a concept. In Laval both parents and children must assume some responsibility for their own behaviour, something most other schools just simply won't allow.

Why in the world are we so reluctant to show a child how to make toast, or pour milk over his own cornflakes? Why are we so fearful of teaching a little bit of self-reliance?

It wouldn't be so bad if at the very least we, instead of pouring milk over the student's cornflakes for them, insisted that they do it themselves. In other words, at the very least don't make breakfast for the kids, show them how to make their own. As things stand now in most of our schools, the children don't even have to pick up their dishes and stick them in a dishwasher after eating.

We've got students as old as 11 and 12 coming to schools, sitting down with their buds in the morning. A volunteer asks them what they want, butters the toast for them, cooks the eggs for them, pours the milk over their cornflakes, does everything for them except spoon the stuff into their little mouths. The kid bolts down the food, gets up without even saying thank you and heads for class or in some cases a smoke! What a wonderful lesson we have just taught. Quite possibly the only lesson they learned all day.

If you are one of those who thinks pouring milk over kid's cornflakes for them in school each morning is a good idea, could you please take just a few minutes and kindly explain to me what I don't understand. Very clearly, in the minds of many dear souls who clap for the granola-crunching, tree-hugging, thug huggers, I very badly need to be straightened out on this. So straighten me out please for heaven's sake, because I just don't understand how absolving both parents and children from the minor responsibility of making their own breakfast makes for better parents or children.

Apparently, however, it makes better Liberals and Dippers. You might also explain to me why that is a good thing.

Chapter 13

Low Expectations

A couple of parents were grumbling a bit the other day about coaches of a local novice hockey team pushing the kids too hard. "There're only seven and eight years old," was the complaint, "I don't think they should expect so much of them."

The criticism centred around a pep talk one of the coaches administered prior to a tournament game played at the Bell Sensplex in suburban Kanata. "There's absolutely no reason you can't win this tournament," he told the boys. "We expect you to play as hard as you can; we expect you to do the things we have taught you and we expect you to win!" Which, by the way, is exactly what they did. They did play as hard as they were capable of. They did do the things they had been taught. They were told they were expected to win and they went out, lived up to those expectations and won. In the process, the kids had a ball and learned an important lesson or two about life.

Whether the complaining parents learned anything is doubtful, because sadly, the belief that we shouldn't push our kids too hard or saddle them with high expectations has become almost orthodoxy in this country.

We see it everywhere, especially in our schools, where even in the playgrounds these days the crazy left wing idea that no one is allowed to lose is rapidly gaining traction, which means, of course that no one is allowed to win.

Why we insist on doing this is a complete mystery, because the facts stare us in the face. Kids need to be challenged. They need to be pushed. They need to be told we have high expectations of them. They've got to be motivated to do their best work and to learn. There must be rewards for accomplishments and consequences for lack of accomplishments. To pretend there are no winners and no losers in life is a lie that does children a great disservice.

Think back to your days in school. Where did you learn the most? Which teachers did you respect the most? Where did you learn little or nothing?

Unless you are different from most of us, you did your best in classes where the teachers pushed you the hardest; where there were high expectations and where there were consequences for lack of effort. Conversely, the teachers who didn't expect very much of you probably got just that—not very much.

Let's be honest. With rare exception the teachers who demanded the most of you were the ones where you learned the most, and while you may not have liked those demanding teachers very much they are probably the ones you respected the most and the ones you remember most fondly today.

Unfortunately there are many of us with conservative convictions who believe the entire public school system is heading in exactly the wrong direction today. The same education "experts" who gave us "new math" which pretty well guaranteed that no kid could make change for a dollar; the same ones who scrapped phonics in favor of the "whole word" system that pretty well destroyed an entire generation's ability to read properly are now preaching what appears to be education parity.

This new "progressive" method is a feel-good kind of instruction that ensures no student ever feels badly about themselves. This, we are assured, feeds the student's ego. Self-esteem, they claim, is enhanced. Competition must not be allowed, even in the schoolyard or playing fields because it means there will be winners and losers and losing hurts people's feelings and heaven only knows we can't go around hurting people's feelings! At least that's what the eggheads who dream these fictions up are claiming.

What all this results in is that the pursuit of any kind of academic excellence must be discouraged because it only ensures that some students will do better than others and there come those hurt feelings again.

Learning must be subordinated to the great "progressive" ideal of academic egalitarianism.

One of the most damaging aspects of all of these beliefs is that children know very well where they stand in the pecking order of ability and accomplishment. When a child receives a passing grade on an assignment they know does not deserve it, they lose respect for the teacher who gave them this false mark, the school that allows it, and education itself. The passing mark is a blatant lie and the child knows it; understands full well that he or she is being rewarded for something they do not deserve. This does not build self-esteem, in fact some would argue that this kind of falsehood creates cynicism and confusion in the child; it does not make them feel better about themselves. Just the opposite. Any child with a conscience actually feels bad because he or she believes they have cheated.

If we are really concerned about a child's feelings, what about the student who really knows his or her stuff? The one who aces the exam only to learn the kid sitting next to them who never cracked a book gets rewarded with a passing grade? If we're aiming for an egalitarian education system with no winners or losers, what's the incentive to do well? If you can't win or lose what's the sense of even trying for heaven's sake?

One of the skills young people today seem to be losing is the ability to cope with the vicissitudes of life. All their lives they have been protected from any form of adversity, so when they enter the real world with its real problems, disappointments, heartbreaks and defeats they are lost. The coping skills that those of my generation had to acquire merely to survive the rough and tumble of school life have never been learned. Some psychologists believe this is one of the prime reasons for the very disturbing increase in teen suicides. Over-protection has left them vulnerable to the bitter pills that life presents to us all.

Making sure no one is allowed to excel, that all students pass with pretty much the same grade is very harmful. Human nature is such that in real life some people just do better than others. This is very hard for those "progressive" people on the left to admit even though they themselves, by describing themselves as progressive, clearly believe the rest of us are regressive.

In other words the left honestly believes that in the great competition of life they are the clear winners and the rest of us are sorry losers indeed. Figure that one out! On the other hand, we conservatives know full well that the world is full of winners and losers although if the truth were known there are probably fewer losers on the conservative side because, let's face it, we are the ones with our heads screwed on straight.

Chapter 14

Failing to Fail

I'm not sure what other provinces have done to ensure that no student is faced with the possibility of failing or even doing poorly, but in Ontario they fixed that problem very easily. When province-wide testing showed more than a few weak spots and heaven forbid, not only were some students doing better than others, but eek, some schools were doing better than others, they simply lowered the standards so it was virtually impossible for anyone to fail. In fact today, Ontario boasts about twice as many "A" students per capita as any other province.

Premier McGuinty has gone so far as to claim that fully 50 per cent of students graduating from high school scored 80 per cent or better on their exams. Any statistician will tell you such an accomplishment is statistically impossible unless standards are extremely low. As another example of what the province has done, consider the fact that 28,000 more grade six students met or exceeded provincial standards in 2010 compared to the year 2000. Are Ontario children really getting all that much smarter or is it just a whole lot easier to appear smarter today?

The same thing is happening in the United States. Most states, up until recently, insisted that a student achieve at least a C-minus grade average in order to pass into a higher grade. Education "experts" however have long complained that C-minus is asking too much of children today, so in more than a dozen states the passing level has been dropped to D-minus.

According to an article in *The Globe and Mail* (July 18, 2011), researchers Stuart Rojstaczer and Christopher Healy "collected historical data on letter grades awarded by more than 200 four-year colleges and universities," says *The New York Times*. "Their analysis (published in the Teachers College Record) confirm that the share of A grades awarded has skyrocketed over the years. ...Most recently, about 43 per cent of all letter grades given were A's, an increase of 28 percentage points since 1960 and 12 percentage points since 1988. The distribution of B's has stayed relatively constant; the growing share of A's instead comes at the expense of a shrinking share of C's, D's and F's. In fact, only about 10 per cent of grades awarded are D's and F's."

Let me ask you, when our schools begin to lower their standards is that really in the best interests of our children or our nation? How wise is it to lower our standards in the face of growing global competition from countries where education standards are already much higher than ours?

You really have to ask yourself if the real intent here is to educate our children or is social engineering underway? Lowering standards in order to level the playing field is, after all, part of the paternalistic attitude of the socialists. Their gospel is that we have to take care of people whether they require it or not, because, they insist, we really are incapable of looking after ourselves. And by taking care of us, whether we want it or not, they are able to convince many that the answer to all our problems is more government. We are discouraged from overcoming obstacles. Success must be punished with higher taxes; red tape must ensure that no one gets too far ahead of anyone else.

Starting this in our schools fosters students' dependency on others, especially bigger and bigger government. It's a disease that is spreading rapidly everywhere in the country. Think of creeping socialism and soft-on-crime policies and their effects on young people. And while you are at it, please note the ringing endorsement British Prime Minister David Cameron is receiving for finally bucking up his courage and adopting some real Conservative policies. Sixteen thousand bobbies on the streets, more than a thousand arrests, hundreds tossed into jail almost overnight—now that's the way a true Conservative deals with the rioting, looting, smashing and burning that took place in the UK in August 2011. And surprise, surprise, it was the "get tough on the punks" direct action that finally stopped the riots after three days and nights of liberal "feel-good, please be nice now, boys and girls, group-hug" approach that didn't seem to work too well! Let's hope that Cameron, and the entire country for that matter, remember you can hug a thug all you want, but what you'll get in return every time is a good swift kick where it hurts the most.

I would imagine the good folk in Vancouver wish they had a few conservatives running their justice system. Months after the rioting, looting and burning that took place there after the Stanley Cup final in June 2011, there still isn't a single charge laid as of our publication date, despite the fact some of the looters actually confessed. The Liberals very clearly have their heads screwed on backwards so badly they can't even accept a confession!

Chapter 15

Something for Nothing

But, of course, making the students do anything for themselves—even something as simple as making their own toast—is not what this is all about. What's really going on here in these "breakfast clubs" is an object lesson in dependency. We're grooming our children to be good little soldiers for the nanny state.

Please, please. No self-reliance can be taught in this school. This is the place, after all, where we will not fail you no matter how little work you do. We will not insist that you complete assignments on time, indeed if you really don't feel like it, you don't ever have to complete the assignment. We'll pass you anyway. Failure to do so doesn't look good on the school's record. And above all else, we will not do anything, anything at all, that might irritate your parents because, God forbid one of them might launch an objection with one of those wonderful Liberal inventions—a human rights commission—and you know what will be in the fan and who's going to have to pay!

If you think I am not being serious, consider what happened in Montreal not long ago when a seven-year-old schoolboy, recently arrived in Canada made so much noise while eating his free breakfast that he disturbed his classmates. When a monitor told him he was eating like a pig, his parents took it to the Quebec Human Rights Tribunal that awarded the family $17,000 in damages.

The message this shouts to our children is that the state is your nanny. You don't need to do anything. You don't even have to exhibit good manners! Your parents don't need to do anything. The state, in this case the school, will look after you and you don't have to lift a finger. The message is loud and clear. You can't rely on your family, you can't rely on your parents and most of all you can't rely on yourself. The state will take care of you. The state is the place where you can get something for nothing!

Small wonder they are telling us that kids today are more depressed than at any time in history. You keep telling a child they are incapable of doing anything on their own, that they are pretty useless and shouldn't even try anything as arduous as making their own breakfast, well, pretty soon they are going to believe it.

Among other things, we are robbing children of an opportunity to acquire coping skills, a lack of which will seriously handicap the child in later life. Some psychologists believe an inability to cope with problems that burden every life may be contributing to the increasing rate of teenage stress, depression and perhaps, as I said earlier, even suicide.

I don't know about you, but if I thought I really wasn't capable of even making my own breakfast I'd be pretty bloody depressed too. Because the subtle message being transmitted to the child, even the older ones, is that they are incapable of carrying out the simplest of tasks. Self-reliance is pounded out of their heads.

The message it sends to society as a whole is that capitalism (often called "the system") has failed so badly that our communities are filled with people so poor they cannot even provide breakfast for their children. This of course means we need to send more money to government to look after those who can't find the box of cornflakes in the morning. Not only that, but under no circumstances can we even suggest that parents should be questioned, let alone cited for not providing this most important meal of the day.

Irresponsibility is thus rewarded. Don't do your job as a parent? No problem! It's obvious that society hasn't treated you fairly. Capitalism (the system) has failed you. There's nothing you can do to feed your child breakfast. You are helpless, victimized, marginalized. The nanny state will do it for you, but you hard-working people out there who do feed your children breakfast—this terrible injustice is all your fault, so you'd better fork over more of your tax dollars.

Something for nothing doesn't come cheap you know.

Because you see, to the left, compassion means expanding the dependency cycle.

I recall a few years ago, then-NDP Premier of Ontario, Bob Rae, boasted about the amount of welfare money the province was doling out. To the socialists, compassion is measured by the number of people accepting public assistance. They honestly believe you gauge compassion by the number of people on welfare. The more people at the government trough, the more compassionate the state.

When Progressive Conservative Premier Mike Harris finally came along to rescue a province on the verge of bankruptcy, one of the first things he did was lower welfare payments by about 20 per cent. As you can imagine, the howls of protest were long and loud. Some of the NDP's bright lights even predicted riots in the street and people dying in snow banks. Honest. It's on the record!

So what happened?

Well within one year the welfare rolls in Ontario dropped by about 200,000. Almost all got jobs. There were no riots. No one died in a snow bank because they couldn't get welfare. In fact in his first four years as Premier, the Mike Harris government oversaw an increase of 700,000 jobs. In those four years Ontario's welfare rolls were cut in half. He introduced "workfare" that prompted thousands of people who had never worked a day in their lives to go out and get a job.

When you stop and think about it, Mike Harris finds himself in some very interesting conservative company.

Because it took a very conservative president, Ronald Reagan, to launch the longest run of prosperity in the history of the United

States and in his spare time he managed to get the Ruskies to "tear down that wall!"

It took conservative Rudy Giuliani only four years to rescue bankrupt, crime-ridden, filthy, poverty-stricken New York City from decades of left wing liberal administration. In that time he turned New York from the most dangerous city in North America into the safest major city in the United States.

And it took Progressive Conservative Mike Harris about that same length of time to re-energize a basket case of a province back into the country's greatest economic engine.

Despite all of this, in left wing circles in Canada and the United States, the myth persists that these three conservatives, just like all conservatives, were cruel, semi-dumb people who did terrible things. The left still likes to blame Mike Harris because a couple guys up in Walkerton, Ontario, became "befuddled" about proper methods of keeping drinking water safe.

You've got to remember, as far as the media are concerned, when things go wrong it's always the fault of a conservative someplace. Harris should have been up there sampling that water himself making sure it was safe to drink.

But why would we be surprised? After all, the idea that there is no personal responsibility (unless you are a conservative) and we all deserve something for nothing (welfare) is what we're teaching our children during those free school breakfasts. A free pass on your grades, a free breakfast, free rent, free groceries, free beer. Heck, when you get a bit older how about free condoms, free needles, free crack pipes and lots and lots of free sex!

As long as you keep leftists in power the government will always look after you. The nanny state will take over. You didn't bother to study for the exam? We can't fail you because it would make you feel bad. You can't find a job that you feel you are entitled to? No problem, we'll just take a bit more from the working stiffs to give to you.

Society has failed you. And it's all society's fault. That's *us* folks!

And by the way, anyone who tries to deny you all of this something-for-nothing is a bad person who is victimizing you. Probably a Conservative or one of their knuckle-dragging supporters.

All of this provides a wonderful springboard for the CBC and the rest of the left wing media to bombard us with stories about how we need even higher taxes to fund more do-good, social engineering programs and in the process punish the rich for being…well, rich. The media have become expert in exaggerating the magnitude of their pet causes/problems by labelling them crises. Everything is a crisis these days. A crisis that requires what? You guessed it—more government intervention. (Translation: more taxpayer's money.)

Nothing illustrates this better than the "crisis" of homelessness.

Chapter 16

One National Disaster After Another!

On October 28, 1998, a headline appeared in Toronto newspapers declaring: HOMELESSNESS IS A NATIONAL DISASTER. The stories quoted a resolution approved by the far left wing Toronto City Council.

As I told you several years ago in my book *How the granola-crunching, tree-hugging thug huggers are wrecking our country!*, the media went wild. Stories flooded newspapers, radio and TV newscasts featuring "experts," social activists, university professors and bucketfuls of others employed in the mammoth homeless industry. All claimed that yes Toronto City Council was correct; homelessness is a national disaster. There were reports of as many as 25,000 homeless in Toronto alone. As if by magic, the figure soon shot up to 50,000.

Some commentators solemnly maintained there were as many as a quarter million Canadians, including children and pregnant women, sleeping on Canadian streets every night. Talk shows were jammed with outrageous indignation and demands that government do something. (Translation: throw lots more money at the problem.)

Not to be left outdone by the "Big Smoke" far left wing, Ottawa City Councillors Wendy Byrne and Alex Munter presented a motion to Regional Council declaring—you guessed it—HOMELESSNESS IS A NATIONAL DISGRACE. The government has got to do something! (Translation: throw lots more money at the problem).

There followed similar declarations by city councils across the country. I was able to count 27 different declarations within the space of two months all saying essentially the same thing—HOMELESSNESS IS A NATIONAL DISGRACE. The word crisis in relation to homelessness has appeared in almost every daily newspaper in Canada countless times. Each time, there were demands that the government do something. (Translation: drown the damn problem with more and more money.)

Each time we discover to our shock and awe that HOMELESSNESS IS A NATIONAL DISGRACE, or HOMELESSNESS IS A CRISIS, millions more tax dollars pour in from all levels of government. (Translation: from our pockets.)

In an eight-year period from 1998 to 2006 almost $4 billion was pumped into the homeless industry by the provinces and the federal government. That figure does not include the hundreds of millions kicked in by municipalities or the money that came in through various charities. The City of Ottawa, for example, contributes $45 to put a homeless person up in a shelter for one night. Charities provide an additional $10 a night.

As just one example of the manner in which all of this money is just swallowed up by the giant maw of the bottomless pit called the "homeless industry" consider this little endeavour.

In December of 1999, the Federal Government announced it was investing $753 million over three years under something called the National Homeless Initiative (NHI). This was supposed to alleviate or prevent homelessness.

Where did the money go? No one seems to know. But you and I have a pretty good idea don't we? Would you doubt me if I suggested that almost every cent of that money—and most of the rest of the billions we continue yanking from our pockets supposedly to help the homeless— instead disappeared directly into the pockets of armies of social activists, pollsters, researchers, programmers, analysts, professors, psychiatrists…you get it.

Would you be shocked out of your gourd if we learned that the great bulk of all that money went to pay for conferences, round table discussions, studies, information sessions, inquiries, studies of the studies, travel to distant places, more conferences, studies, workshops, more studies, more conferences, and so on and so on? You get the picture! Would you question, even for a brief moment, my suspicions that very little, if any, of that money ever trickled down to the homeless? Ah, I can see by the expression on your face, you think my assumptions are probably correct. I mean, how many homeless people do you see driving around in Caddies?

But the story doesn't end with the missing $753 million from the feds. Because in order to top that figure up, the provinces and municipalities kicked in an additional $553 million. It too just very mysteriously disappeared into the misty fog of a burgeoning bureaucracy.

Three years later, in 2002, the federal government took another $403 million from us and threw it at the homeless industry, followed by another $680 million to provide cheap housing to build 40,000 new so-called affordable housing units. That was matched by the provinces to the tune of another $680 million. But have any houses actually been built with this money?

Who knows? At one point I was told that about 2,200 low-cost homes had actually been built, or might soon be built, or were planned on being built sometime. Maybe. What's your guess? Where do you think all that money disappeared?

I ask you, has any of this money actually taken any homeless people off the streets?

Maybe someplace, but in Vancouver, Calgary, Toronto and Ottawa, where I was able to compare figures, the fact is there are about the same number of homeless people today as there were back in 1999 when that HOMELESSNESS IS A NATIONAL DISGRACE headline first appeared.

Remember the claim of 50,000 homeless in Toronto? Well, on April 19, 2006, some 1,100 eager social activists fanned out across that city to conduct the first ever census of the homeless. They checked every shelter, every church basement, every nook and cranny where the homeless congregate and to the horror of the lefties they could only find 5,052. This in a city of more than five million. Not only that, but lo and behold there was actually plenty of space for all of the 5,052 in the City's various shelters. In fact, although it was a very cold night, there were several hundred empty beds in various shelters and such is the case every night in Toronto.

There were claims that the counters must have missed some, but later reviews indicated they probably counted some of the homeless more than once. Don't forget those employed in the "homeless industry" get paid by the head. In other words, so much money per homeless person. So you can imagine the frantic efforts to find as many of these dollar producers as possible. Much to the chagrin of the social activists, they had to conclude that there were, in fact, fewer than 5,000 homeless in Toronto and shockingly enough, about one quarter of them were aboriginal, for whom taxpayer-funded homes would be available on their reserves.

The census threw shock waves into the homeless industry in the GTA because, only weeks prior, the city handed over $160 million to a multitude of social agencies to "fix" the homeless problem. Unless my math is way off, that works out to about $31,000 per year per actual homeless person in Toronto. Plus of course the millions of dollars donated via various charities. In Ottawa the figure is about $35,000 per year per homeless person on top of charitable donations. As far as we can determine the $160 million didn't get a single homeless person off Toronto streets.

But perhaps the saddest thing about all of this is the fact that an estimated 40 per cent of those who are legitimately homeless have a serious mental illness that tragically often goes untreated because of left-wing ideology. A tragic misguided ideology that believes any attempt to insist that seriously ill people receive medical treatment contravenes their right to wander the streets in a fog of confusion and paranoia. Most of those working with the homeless today refuse to force a mentally ill person into hospital even though such action could very well save that person's life.

Let me provide just one example of what I'm talking about.

For years a wonderfully talented young Ottawa man battled schizophrenia. For more than five years he was in and out of hospitals. At one point, thinking aliens were attacking him, he leaped from a second story window.

Although tremendously talented and artistic he wandered the streets, often going days without eating. On one occasion he was rushed to hospital in Ottawa and was on the road to recovery thanks to some very effective medical treatment. His recovery, however, came crashing to a halt when one of Bob Rae's volunteer "counsellors" visited the young man in hospital and advised him that he didn't have to stay in hospital and he didn't have to take his medication.

Confused, the young man came to believe the "counsellor" was his lawyer and that his parents were trying to destroy him. He fled the hospital and for another two years wandered the streets, often being rushed to various hospital emergency wards as his health continued to deteriorate. Always he was allowed to leave hospital when he wanted no matter how confused and dangerous to himself he was. That was the law of the land.

More than a year later, this time thanks to "Brian's Law" which allowed his parents to have him hospitalized for 72 hours due to mental and physical deterioration, he began to respond to treatment and appeared to be on his way to recovery when he read an article that quoted the Canadian Mental Health Association stating their official position that mental patients should not have to receive medical assistance if they did not choose to do so.

Once again the young man, believing his parents and doctors were trying to harm him, fled the hospital, and for more than a year flirted with death. The father was so incensed that he contacted the Ottawa office of the Canadian Mental Health Association, told them the damage their position was doing and threatened to bring his son down to their office so they could deal with him. The Association expressed no sympathy and offered no support.

Thank heavens that finally, once again thanks to "Brian's Law" and very persistent and loving parents, the young man was hospitalized, underwent treatment and today is an extremely productive member of society in a very responsible job. No one would suspect he had ever been ill.

Not once was the family provided any support by any of the social agencies in the community. The hospitals and doctors did their level best, so did the Ottawa Police Department and the family but not a single agency we pay to help the homeless lifted a finger to offer any support, any advice or any help at any stage of the illness other than a pittance disability benefit of less than one thousand dollars a month for a brief period.

The story is repeated countless times across the country every day.

But I'm getting ahead of myself here so let me explain about these so-called mental health counsellors and "Brian's Law."

One of the most destructive things Bob Rae did during his tenure as Premier of Ontario was turn thousands of mentally ill patients out of hospitals and institutions onto the streets. Believe it or not, he then appointed a small army of totally unqualified so-called counsellors to visit every hospital in the province and advise every mentally ill patient still being treated that they did not have to remain there and did not have to take any medication. Even more incredibly these "counsellors" or "patient advocates" as they were sometimes called, also gave the same advice to elderly Alzheimer's patients in various nursing homes. Lives were shattered and lost because of it.

It was classic left wing ideology gone completely mad.

On one occasion, a young man strapped to a bed in Ottawa's Queensway Carleton Hospital, after going berserk and throwing billiard balls through a wall, was approached by one of these "counsellors" who told him the doctors had no legal right to keep him in hospital. Despite the pleas of doctors, nurses and the young man's family, he was released and bolted from the room. God only knows what happened to him. When the "counsellor" was confronted by the angry father he was told that since the young man was over the age of 14 it was none of his [the father's] business!

Under the Bob Rae socialist government that is what was considered compassion.

One of those lives lost because of this "compassion" was that of Ottawa athlete and sportscaster Brian Smith who was shot and killed by a man who, because he was not required to take medication, heard voices telling him to kill the first media personality he recognized.

The dreaded Conservative, Premier Mike Harris, lobbied by Brian's widow and others, including me, passed what we now call "Brian's Law" that allows us to hospitalize patients who are seriously mentally ill for up to 72 hours when they exhibit mental and/or physical deterioration. It's not nearly long enough to get many patients stabilized, but it is a first step and it does help. Brian's Law was and still is being fought every step of the way by the left wing ideologues.

Tragically, many of the people we see living in despair could be living normal or near normal lives if only those same ideologues would show real compassion and make sure the people they are being paid to assist get the kind of help that would actually get them off the streets. That is, get them into hospital where they can receive proper treatment.

Some of the modern drugs come as close to performing miracles as you can get. They can stabilize a seriously ill patient in a few days and with proper care and support it often takes only a few months, or even a few weeks to get them back to living a normal or near normal life with few if any side effects.

There are thousands of people living very productive lives today because somewhere along the way someone cared enough to insist they get treatment and helped them do so. On the other hand there are thousands of others who sadly have no home because the people who are supposed to look after them allow left wing ideology to overrule common sense and real compassion.

Of course there's another reason we don't get mentally ill people the treatment that would get them off the streets.

If we got everyone off the streets, what would those involved in the giant homeless industry do for a living?

Chapter 17

The Great Low-cost Housing Shell Game

You can hardly pick up a newspaper these days, watch a TV newscast or listen to radio without hearing the plaintive cry from the left that we must have more low-cost housing. Many cities have imposed zoning bylaws that require developers to devote a certain percentage of the houses they build for low-income people. The late Jack Layton and his wife even enjoyed the "low-cost" lifestyle in Toronto for a time.

"Affordable housing" is a left wing mantra.

But let me explain why it is the left wing demand for more and more social programs and more and more low-skilled immigrants that are two of the primary reasons that constructing so-called affordable housing is becoming more difficult by the day.

One of Canada's leading land developers is Ottawa's Roger Greenberg, CEO of the Minto Group, one of the country's largest homebuilders and a prime mover of a plan to revitalize Ottawa's iconic Lansdowne Park and bring back CFL football to the Capital.

In a recent address to the Greater Ottawa Home Builders' Association, Greenberg pointed out that housing is now the third highest taxed item in Ontario, behind only alcohol and cigarettes. "When did housing become a sin?" he asked, then proceeded to back up his statement with cold hard facts.

"In recent years there's been an incredible increase in government-imposed charges through fees, taxes and levies," he explained. "Twenty-five years ago, government-imposed charges totalled less than five per cent of the cost of building a home. Today that cost has ballooned to between 20 and 30 per cent. That is one of the main reasons the cost of housing is being driven up."

Can you imagine? Twenty to 30 per cent of home building costs today are taxes, fees and levies.

So the next time your favourite politician demands that we provide more affordable housing, just remember, it's those kinds of demands for more and more social assistance, for bigger and bigger governments, more and more programs at every level, that is making housing of all kinds less and less affordable.

The "progressives" flail away at "greedy capitalist developers," and of course hard-hearted conservatives everywhere for what they claim is a lack of caring about the poor. But when you examine what's really happening, lo and behold, it turns out the greediest of them all are the three levels of government and their insatiable thirst for more and more money which, rather than helping people put a roof over their heads, are taxing people out from under the roof they already have.

All of this, let's never forget, to meet the demands of the socialists and liberals who believe governments should be looking after us all from cradle to grave.

But there's another aspect to this affordable housing shortage that very few want to talk about. Let's face the facts and tell the truth. Most of the pressure for low-cost housing in Canada is because of our mass immigration policy.

If you read my book *Mayday! Mayday!* you know that Canada is not producing enough babies to replace the people who die. Thus it doesn't take a mental giant to realize that the main reason we need more housing is because of pressure from the more than 300,000 newcomers who immigrate to Canada each year. Plus more than a quarter million "temporary" workers and more than 100,000 foreign students, all of whom need a place in which to live.

There are other factors—populations move from one location to another and boomers are starting to downsize are a couple of examples—but if you do the math you realize that without immigration, overall, Canada really wouldn't need many new houses. A declining population doesn't put a lot of pressure on the housing market.

But that's only part of the picture, because when you really dig into the facts you find that these days in our major cities, almost all the demand for affordable housing comes from recent arrivals who don't have the training, education or language skills to obtain a well-paid job. Cultural differences, as well, are often an impediment to employment.

Before 1961, only 6.8 per cent of our immigrant population lived below the poverty line, but from 1996 until 2001 (the last year for which we have figures) the number of immigrants living below the poverty line jumped to an astonishing and very disturbing 41.2 per cent. In comparison, during that same period, only 11.2 per cent of non-immigrants were living below the poverty line.

To give you an even clearer picture, according to Statistics Canada, during that period between 1996 and 2001, 23.4 per cent of American immigrants, 33.7 per cent of immigrants from Europe, 44.6 per cent of immigrants from Asia and an incredible 48.8 per cent of immigrants from Africa were living below the poverty line.

When you see figures like that you quickly realize who it is that needs most of our low-cost housing, which begs the question, why are we bringing such large numbers of people into Canada who don't have the skills or education that will give them at least a decent chance at a good living? If anyone can figure that one out please let me know!

So we've got the "progressive" left wing demanding more social programs and higher taxes for the housing industry while at the same time insisting that we maintain and even increase the numbers of low-skilled immigrants coming to Canada.

All of it creating higher costs and more demand. Thank heavens we conservatives, with our heads screwed on straight understand this astonishing fact.

Most of the demand for low-cost housing is being imported from other countries.

And the incredible part is, if you ask the lefty crowd who's at fault for a shortage of low-cost housing, they'll be quick to tell you it's we mean-spirited conservatives who keep agitating for lower taxes.

Chapter 18

Why Social Agencies Never Solve a Social Problem

Don't get me wrong here. There are all kinds of wonderfully concerned and compassionate people involved in social agencies of all kinds. Good people who honestly want to save the world, or at least rescue a few marginalized, victimized domestic refugees from the evil, greedy, globalized, capitalist, corporate world created by non-progressive conservatives. (Is there any other kind?)

The problem is that most of those involved in social work today got their heads badly turned around in our left-wing universities and have never been able to get those heads screwed back on straight. Nice people for the most part, but badly confused. And of course they must all be terribly torn.

Because, let's tell the truth here, if any of the social agencies ever solved the problems they are supposed to, all their employees would be out of work.

Come on now. Can you think of a single agency within the massive poverty industry that has ever solved a problem? Because if they did, they would have to disband. Quickly now, name me one government bureaucracy that has been so successful at solving a problem that it shut itself down? You can't even imagine it happening can you?

Those who work in the welfare bureaucracy have a vested interest in making sure conditions never improve. In fact, if conditions worsen, the welfare bureaucracy expands. It's one of the main reasons that no matter how the country's economy improves, the welfare lists grow longer. No matter how much money we shovel into the homeless "problem" hardly any of the homeless ever get a home.

And it's not just in the poverty industry either.

Let me ask you this: Does adding more heads of departments, assistant heads of departments, assistants to the assistants, supervisors, chiefs of various stripes and odours result in better health care? When they add more offices to your favourite hospital and fill them with PhDs does it result in shorter wait times for any medical procedure? I rest my case!

I will never forget what a young nurse told me during a book signing in Brockville. "Lowell," she said, "the problem in our hospitals today is too many high heels and not enough running shoes!"

One of the things that was clearly illustrated when Bob Rae and his socialist friends took over in Ontario was that the more "goodies" that are handed out, the more people will be there with their hands out. And of course more goodies mean lots more highly paid people are needed to do the handing out.

When Rae virtually doubled welfare payments guess what happened? Surprise, surprise! The number of welfare recipients more than doubled. So did the number of social workers and the necessary administrative bureaucracy.

As I have already pointed out, when Mike Harris cut welfare payments by 20 per cent some 200,000 people left the welfare rolls and got jobs. The sad part is, even when Harris managed to get welfare rolls cut almost in half, as soon as Liberals took over at the provincial and municipal levels, the number of government employees required to service those still on the dole remained constant. Indeed in some communities, Ottawa, for example, with a former Liberal cabinet minister as mayor, we somehow managed to substantially increase the number of social workers and the welfare bureaucracy. We even expanded their office space, ending up with essentially about double the number of employees in double the space to service a caseload about half the size. Amazing isn't it? I knew you would be really, really surprised!

That's bad enough, but what I have found over the years is that when real help is needed it most likely will not come from the institutionalized or unionized state-run bureaucracies, but rather from volunteer and charitable agencies such as the Salvation Army. You cannot believe the number of calls I receive from desperate people in need of help of all kinds, who, despite the billions we pour into the poverty industry can find no one to even steer them in the right direction.

I suspect what happened to one of my favorite uncles many years ago is the best illustration of why we can't seem to solve the home-less problem, or the drug problem, or the health care problem, or any social problem.

Ken Green for several years was the Executive Director of the London, Ontario, Drug and Alcohol Addiction Research Foundation. It was a good job, well-paid with lots of prestige and security for the father of a growing family. One day Ken just walked out of his office and never came back. He took a hike up to northern Ontario and started a maple syrup operation, something he had no experience in whatsoever. He was struggling mightily to make ends meet when I went up to see him one day. "Ken," I asked, "what in the world were you thinking, leaving a job like that?" I'll never forget his answer. "Lowell, we became ex-perts at holding wonderful conferences, meetings and discussions. We met with experts of all kinds and our workshops were the envy of many. The only problem was, when a drunk walked through our doors looking for help we had no idea how to deal with him."

If you think that's an isolated case consider what happened in 1995 when a three-day workshop was held at the University of Toronto to discuss how to carry out a proper head count of the homeless. Yes that's right, a three-day workshop involving a panel of experts from the United States and Canada just to define exactly what constitutes a homeless person. Let me quote directly from a review of the workshop written by T. Peressini, PhD, L. McDonald, PhD and D. Hulchanski, PhD. Keep in mind as you read this please; it took three PhDs to compose the following:

> *The Workshop on Homelessness brought together a panel of experts from the United States and Canada to critically review the various definitions and methods that are currently available, and to offer recommendations concerning those that are preferred or optimal. The panel consisted of experts from government, the service community, the research community and academia.*

> *On the first day of the workshop the issue of the types of definitions of homeless that should be used was discussed and debated. Participants emerged from this debate agreeing that researchers prefer definitions that are focused on the literally homeless. These types of definitions are chosen because they are relatively easy to operationalize and implement and they provide the highest return in terms of cost effectiveness and representation of the population.*

Incredible as it may seem, some of the brightest and highest-paid people in the land struggled for an entire day just trying to figure out how to define "homeless person." At the end of that day they finally agreed that a homeless person was a person who did not have a home in which to live. Amazing!

The next two days were just as incredibly nonsensical. At the end of this mighty endeavour they concluded—surprise, surprise—that more funding was required and a committee was formed to further study the problem of counting the homeless. (You can't make this stuff up!)

The last time I checked, the giant brains involved in all of this con-centrated stupidity still had not agreed on how to count the home-less. The money spent thus far on this incredibly difficult task (for PhDs) would undoubtedly have provided homes for dozens of the homeless. (People without homes!)

Just for the heck of it, Google "homeless studies Ontario." Incredi-bly, up will pop about 2.7 million results. As best I can determine, during the past 20 years there have been at least 7,000 studies of the "homeless problem" in Ontario. The number of people, including some of the best educated in the country that have taken part in these studies is estimated to be in excess of 25,000. Heaven only knows the numbers for all of Canada, or the cost of all of this.

I suspect we could build a lovely little one-bedroom condo for every homeless person in Canada for a fraction of what we have spent on studies of the problem. If anyone cares to dispute this you know how to get in touch with me.

Well, I can hear you say, that's fine and dandy, you've pointed out a few failings of the lefties, but how about giving us some examples of how conservatives have done a better job. Forget "Where's the beef?" Where's the proof we conservatives are the only ones with our heads screwed on straight?

Fair question.

Where to begin?

Chapter 19

Churchill

I f we are looking for proof that only we conservatives have our heads screwed on straight, Winston Churchill's head would be a good place to start.

Since most of you reading this book are conservative thinkers and thus well-read with vastly superior intelligence, I hardly need to tell you of the role Winston Churchill played in saving the world from Nazi tyranny. But on the off chance that a few liberals may pick this book and by accident begin reading it, I will fill in a few details.

What many don't know is that Churchill was first elected to the British Parliament in 1900 as a Conservative. He switched to the Liberal Party four years later, but after 20 years of seeing the mess that liberalism was creating in Britain he switched allegiance back to the

Conservative Party. In fact, his views leading up to the start of World War II were considered so conservative that many, including some within his own party, considered him to be a right-wing fanatic.

Thus, as he began to stand in the House of Commons to warn the British Parliament of the storm clouds gathering over Europe he was often jeered and laughed at.

We now know that Churchill had access to secret information he was not supposed to have concerning German war production and preparation but unfortunately hardly anyone took him seriously. As he rose in the House to gravely provide a daily count of the number of tanks and airplanes the Germans had produced in the last 24 hours, many MPs turned their backs on him or walked out. As always the Liberals and the left wing of his own party believed they knew better. Some of them, in fact, believed Hitler was kind of a neat guy.

So when Prime Minister Neville Chamberlain performed his little "peace in our time" jig after returning from Berlin, waving that piece of paper with Hitler's signature firmly affixed, Churchill was vilified. Catcalls of "warmonger" rang out on the street as he passed by. It was a great victory for liberalism. Well for a few days it was!

I won't go through the rest of the story. Even liberals have heard some of Churchill's most famous speeches, such as this one from June 4, 1940:

(Be honest here, can you even conceive of those great and famous Liberals like Bill Clinton, Jimmy Carter or even Barack Obama remaining steadfast and fearless in the face of possible annihilation and rallying his people with words like these?)

> *Even though large tracts of Europe and many old and famous States have fallen or may fall into the grip of the Gestapo and all the odious apparatus of Nazi rule, we shall not flag or fail. We shall go on to the end, we shall fight in France, we shall fight on the seas and oceans, we shall fight with growing confidence and growing strength in the air, we shall defend our Island, whatever the cost may be, we shall fight on the beaches, we shall fight on the landing grounds, we shall fight in the fields and in the streets, we shall fight in the hills; we shall never surrender, and even if, which I do not for a moment believe, this Island or a large part of it were subjugated and starving, then our Empire beyond the seas, armed and guarded by the British Fleet, would carry on the struggle, until, in God's good time, the New World, with all its power and might, steps forth to the rescue and the liberation of the old.*

From a man who only months before was vilified as a right wing fanatic.

But Churchill is not the only conservative who has had to clean up the mess left behind by liberal predecessors.

Chapter 20

The Iron Lady

When Margaret Thatcher took office as Prime Minister in 1979 the previous left wing Labour Government had virtually destroyed the nation. Unemployment soared to more than three million and the International Monetary Fund had to step in to rescue the situation when the value of Britain's currency collapsed. It required tight expenditure controls, which caused the unions to go on a rampage of strikes that almost brought the country to its knees. For a while there was even fear that the unions might carry out some sort of coup and take over the government. Racial tension ramped up to dangerous levels.

As one of her first acts as Prime Minister, Margaret Thatcher reduced immigration and clamped down heavily on the concept of multi-culturalism.

Her approval rating increased 11 per cent overnight during her campaign to become prime minister, when she went on television to say: "The moment a minority threatens to become a big one, people get frightened. The British character has done so much for democracy, for law, that if there is any fear that it might be swamped, people are going to react and be rather hostile to those coming."

The left of course claimed she was a racist.

Her monetary policies, heavily influenced by people like President Ronald Reagan and Milton Friedman, were also heavily criticized, but despite a risk of alienating even her own party she lowered income taxes, increased interest rates to slow the rate of inflation, introduced cash limits on public spending and reduced expenditures on social services such as education and housing.

One of her most famous statements was made during the 1980 Conservative Party conference, where the Party's left wing began agitating for what it called a turn in a different direction. Thatcher's reply: "You turn if you want to. The lady's not for turning!"

Her policies began to work. By 1982 the UK began to experience signs of economic recovery. Inflation dropped to 8.6 per cent from a high of 18 per cent.

Her policy of privatization has been described by many as "a crucial ingredient of Thatcherism." Her sale of state utilities raised more than 29 billion pounds. Another 18 billion pounds was raised when she sold "council houses" (low-rent housing) to the people who were renting them. She was fought every step of the way by those on the left but her biggest battle was with the unions.

In 1984 Thatcher ordered 20 of the state-owned mines that were losing money closed. Two-thirds of the country's miners downed their tools in protest. Steadfast, Thatcher refused to give in, despite screams of protest from all quarters. For one solid year she refused to cave, until finally in March of 1985 the unions admitted defeat and went back to work. Eventually she closed a total of 97 unprofitable pits and then sold off and privatized the rest. The union's chokehold on the nation was finally broken. Many believe she saved the UK from total economic collapse and perhaps even something worse.

The number of work stoppages across the UK had peaked in 1979 when more than 29 million working days were lost through strikes. In 1984, the year of the great miners' strike, there were more than 27 million working days lost. But after the unions admitted defeat, stoppages fell steadily to only two million working days lost in 1990. And continued to fall even after her resignation as Prime Minister on November 28, 1990.

During her term of office Margaret Thatcher reshaped almost every aspect of British life, revived the economy, reformed outdated institutions and reinvigorated the nation's foreign policy. She challenged the psychology of decline that had overtaken much of Britain and spurred the recovery with amazing determination against tremendous odds. She also played a major role, along with Ronald Reagan, in bringing about an end to the Cold War and the destruction of the Berlin Wall.

According to the Margaret Thatcher Foundation:

> *In the process, Margaret Thatcher become one of the founders, with Ronald Reagan, of a school of conservative conviction politics, which has had a powerful and enduring impact on politics in Britain and the United States and earned her a higher international profile than any British politician since Winston Churchill.*
>
> *By successfully shifting British economic and foreign policy to the right, her governments helped to encourage wider international trends which broadened and deepened during the 1980s and 1990s as the end of the Cold War, the spread of democracy and the growth of free markets strengthened political and economic freedom in every continent.*

Still need more evidence that only those of us with conservative convictions have our heads screwed on straight?

Okay then how about the guy who told Gorbachev to "Tear down that wall!"

Chapter 21

The Reagan Revolution

A poll carried out in the US a couple of years ago indicated the two things people remember the most about Ronald Reagan were his famous suggestion to "Tear down that wall, Mr. Gorbachev," and his courage and determination in firing all the striking air traffic controllers.

Until recently, most of his other accomplishments have been buried under an avalanche of negative press from the left wing media and oceans of propaganda from the Democrats.

There is no question that liberals in the US have relentlessly pursued their goal of trying to destroy the legacy of the Reagan presidency. His era has been dubbed the "Decade of Greed." Commentators and editorial writers have sneered at the "trickle down" theory of

Reaganomics. His role in the movie *Bedtime for Bonzo* is dragged out almost every time anyone tries to point to the incredible success he had in pulling the nation out of recession and, perhaps even more importantly, restoring to Americans their pride and belief in themselves following the terrible discord of the Vietnam era and the humiliation of the failed attempt to rescue 52 Americans held captive in Iran for more than a year. In fact the 52 were released even as Reagan was delivering his inaugural address. The Iranians knew they could not thumb their nose at Ronald Reagan as they had at Jimmy Carter!

The reason for the liberal's fear is simple. The Ronald Reagan record represents one of the most dangerous enemies liberalism has ever confronted.

The facts are irrefutable. Ronald Reagan was by far the most truly conservative president the United States has ever had, more conservative even than either of the Bushes, and he is by far the most successful. His legacy destroys every liberal shibboleth. If liberals in America are to have any success they must mask the truth, rewrite history, distort the public record of that period and alter the public's perception of the Reagan legacy.

So let me just very briefly review some of the accomplishments of the godfather of conservative thinking.

Let me issue a warning here. If, even after making it this far in this book of "revelations" you are still tilting towards the left, go no further. Given the state of our government monopoly health care system

I have no wish to crowd emergency wards even more with throngs of confused and panicked people whose lifelong beliefs have been shattered by the truisms of this book!

First and foremost is the fact that the Reagan era ushered in the longest period of peacetime growth in American history—96 consecutive months of non-stop prosperity. Please keep in mind this followed the disastrous economic policies of the left wing Jimmy Carter administration with its 21 per cent interest rates and 14 per cent inflation.

According to the US Bureau of the Census, real income for the average American family fell from 1977 right through until 1981 when Reagan assumed the presidency. With surprising skill he managed to turn the situation around almost immediately with legislation that cut taxes and government expenses, while rebuilding the military.

Here are a few facts provided by the US Census Bureau:

- Average real family income grew by well over 15 per cent from 1982, when Reagan assumed power, until 1989 when he completed his second term in office.

- For the poorest fifth of Americans, real income during his presidency grew almost 12 per cent.

- Families earning more than $50,000 (in 1990 dollars) went from fewer than 25 per cent of families in 1980 to 31 per cent in 1990.

- The percentage of families earning less than $15,000 dropped considerably and, most interesting, between 1983 and 1989 the total number of Americans living under the poverty line decreased by 3.8 million people, and the black middle class with incomes of $25,000 or more grew from 2.6 million households in 1979 to 3.9 million in 1989.

- Almost 20 million new jobs were created during the Reagan era. Amazingly, 82 per cent were in the higher-skilled, higher-paying occupations.

- Between 1982 and 1989, real after-tax income per person rose by 15.5 per cent.

Most of the criticism leveled at Reagan during his tenure centred around his stated goal of "peace through strength." The wits and half-wits on late night television and in Hollywood had a ball with that one. Newspapers led by *The New York Times* and *Washington Post* more than hinted they believed the President was crazy. Remember all the hullabaloo over his "Star Wars" plan?

Defence spending increased 35 per cent under Reagan, which many claimed was scandalous, but we all know what happened don't we? For every ruble the Soviets spent on new weaponry Reagan spent triple or quadruple that amount.

He met them head-on at every turn as they attempted to spread communism throughout Asia, Central America and Africa until Mikhail Gorbachev, realizing that trying to outspend the United States would bankrupt the Soviet Union, finally threw in the towel.

The left would still have you believe that ending the Cold War, tearing down the Berlin Wall and setting tens of millions free of the terrible yoke of communism had little, if anything to do with Reagan. They apparently believe it can all be attributed to "fairy dust" or proper alignment of the stars. What drives them crazy of course is the undeniable fact that it all happened during the tenure of the man many today acknowledge as the father of modern conservatism.

Others, including Margaret Thatcher, certainly played a role in tearing down the Berlin Wall and the Iron Curtain, but as the air traffic controllers learned to their chagrin, the last man in the world you wanted to tangle with was Ronald Reagan and the Russians, recognizing true grit and steel, wisely decided not to even try it.

Let's be honest here. It took Ronald Reagan to finally convince the Russkies to get their heads screwed on straight—partially, at least. Too bad he's not around today to finish the job.

So what have we learned so far? Well how about this:

- Conservative Winston Churchill cleaned up the Nazis!

- Conservative Margaret Thatcher cleaned up the unions!

- Conservative Ronald Reagan cleaned up the communists!

- And then we have the guy who cleaned up New York City!

Chapter 22

Rudy

- In 1943 New York City had a population of 7,472,564.

- In 1993 New York City had a population of 7,322,564.

- In 1943 New York City had 73,000 welfare cases.

- In 1993 New York City had 1,200,000 welfare cases.

- In 1943 New York City recorded 44 gunshot homicides.

- In 1993 New York City recorded 1,499 gunshot homicides.

In September 1990, *Time* magazine ran a cover story headlined "The Rotting of the Big Apple." The story described New York City as the crime and welfare capital of the United States. Violence was out of control. Businesses were fleeing the city by the thousands.

The infrastructure was crumbling. The place was filthy. The police department was riddled with corruption and the city was bankrupt, crying to Washington for enough money to meet the payrolls of their teachers and police.

The *New York Post* carried a headline one day that filled the entire front page asking desperately, "WILL SOMEBODY PLEASE DO SOMETHING?"

To which the far left wing mayor responded bravely: "Yes, I David Dinkins will do something to stop this terrible decline of my city. I am going to remove cigarette advertising from New York phone booths!" Honest to God that was his response! With crime totally out of control, murder such a daily occurrence that the media stopped reporting anything short of a triple homicide, porn shops circling almost every high school in the city, Mayor Dinkins removes cigarette advertising from phone booths. The left wing mind at work.

Oh, I almost forgot to mention one of the other things that Mayor Dinkins did to make New York a safer, warmer, sexier place was introduce a "Teenager's Bill of Rights" in the city's high schools which stated the following:

- *I have the right to decide whether to have sex and who to have it with. I have the right to use protection when I have sex. I have the right to buy and use condoms.*

- *Condoms can be sexy! They come in different colours, sizes, flavors and styles, to be more fun for you and your partner. You can put them on together. Shop around till you find the type you like best. Be creative and be safe. Guys can get used to the feel of condoms while masturbating.*

The campaign was intended to attack the problem of teen pregnancies but when New York was rocked by an increase in sexual harassment in the schools and teen pregnancies actually increased the response from Dinkins and his "progressive" followers was to complain that the program didn't have enough money. The idea that perhaps teaching children that premarital sex is fine and dandy, while refusing any religious instruction, might have something to do with the problem, apparently never entered their poorly screwed-on heads.

As for needing more money, New York State introduced a special program designed to reduce the terrible dropout rate in their schools. So taxpayers forked over $68 million for a program created and administered by some of the state's most eminent educational experts. Two years later the $68 million was all gone and the dropout rate *increased* by five per cent. The explanation offered was they simply didn't have enough money. Sounds familiar doesn't it?

The comparison of New York City statistics from 1943 and 1993 is a powerful illustration of the ravages not of time, but of 50 years of left wing, liberal, soft-on-crime, easy welfare administrations.

For almost all of that 50 years, high-ranking left wing Democrats held a virtual monopoly, not just in New York City but in the entire State. It was they who allowed, in fact aided and abetted, the terrible decline and the cultural and moral degradation that was destroying what was once one of the great cities of the world.

In fact New York City, Washington DC and most other large urban areas north of the Mason-Dixon Line from World War II through to the 90s were bastions of left-wing liberalism and, with rare exceptions, all were being rocked by racial strife, rampant drug use, poverty, crime and filth. It simply was not safe, even during the day, to walk the streets throughout vast areas of most major northern cities with Democrat administrations.

Such was the situation on January 1, 1993, that confronted ultra-conservative Rudy Giuliani, newly elected mayor of New York City and good friend of conservative President Ronald Reagan.

It didn't take Rudy long to go to work and apply some solid conservative common sense solutions. On January 2 he called New York Police Commissioner Bill Bratton into his office and laid down the law. "Clean up the corruption in the police force," he ordered, "clean the streets of panhandlers and drug addicts, and lay charges against everybody for even the most minor crimes."

The next day police began laying jaywalking charges against the small army of squeegee people who had been driving motorists nuts. Within three days the practice stopped and as an added bonus they found that many of those charged were wanted for more serious crimes. Into jail they went.

The next message from Rudy was that no one in New York would be allowed to live on the streets. "You've got three choices," said Rudy, "find a place to live, go into drug or alcohol rehab or go to jail, but you cannot live on the streets. It's unsightly, unsafe and unsanitary."

When police rounded up a few of them the message quickly spread that things had changed in New York and almost overnight most of the street people disappeared.

Charges were laid for the smallest infractions, including against the common practice of jumping over charge styles at subway stops. Those caught spraying graffiti were heavily fined. Building owners were ordered to repair broken windows because, Rudy argued, a broken window indicates to some people that nobody cares. "From now on, we care in New York," he said.

The police department was purged of dozens of cops on the take. Hundreds of new police were hired along with thousands of new teachers. Schools were ordered to strictly enforce discipline; many of the porn shops that used to litter Times Square were shut down.

Every step of the way the leftists screamed and warned that none of it would work. You'll only fill the jails they charged; you'll totally bankrupt the State. It's unconstitutional.

Maybe so, but here's what eight years of conservative common sense was able to accomplish in New York City:

- In 1993 there were 1,946 homicides in New York; a year later, 1994—the year Rudy came to power and instituted his broken windows policy—the number declined almost 20 per cent to 1,561.

- By 2001, the last year of Rudy's administration there were 642 murders in New York city, an incredible reduction of 67 per cent—IN JUST EIGHT YEARS!

- Overall crime was reduced 57 per cent in those eight years.

- Shootings dropped 75 per cent.

- There were almost 1,200 fewer rapes in 2000 compared to 1993.

- Robberies declined from more than 85,000 to just over 36,000.

- Auto theft plummeted from almost 112,000 to fewer than 36,000.

- Burglary dropped from nearly 101,000 to just over 38,000.

But it wasn't just crime that Rudy attacked. The teacher-pupil ratio was greatly improved by the addition of thousands of new teachers.

He built or renovated more than 73,000 low-cost, subsided housing units and acquired more than 2,000 acres of new parkland.

All of this was accomplished while reducing the city payroll by more than 20,000 positions even after adding many more police and teachers and amazingly taxes were reduced more than 15 per cent for homeowners and businesses.

When Rudy took over New York, the city was bankrupt, pleading for help from the federal government. Eight years later, when Rudy moved on, the city had a surplus of almost $3 billion.

Anyone who visited New York prior to 1993 and then again after Rudy left will tell you that they simply did not recognize the city. Almost all the panhandlers were gone—so too the porn shops—and people could stroll the streets at night with no fear. The graffiti was gone, the subway was safe to ride again, the broken windows were fixed, and the city sparkled.

The Big Apple wasn't rotten anymore thanks to just eight years of conservative administration.

If you're interested in learning more about what I call the miracle of New York pick up a copy of Rudy's book *Leadership*. You'll see all the proof you ever need that indeed it is only we conservatives who have our heads screwed on straight.

Fifty years of liberalism to virtually destroy a city. Eight years of conservatism to restore it!

I've raised this miracle story many times on my radio show in Ottawa and almost always some lefty will try and shoot it down. The story the liberals began to spread, even as Rudy was in the midst of cleaning the place up, was that it really wasn't his broken windows theory that fixed things, but rather demographics. People got older in New York they claimed, and as you get older you don't commit as many crimes. Honestly that's the story most liberals will give you today and as usual no one in the mainstream media bothers to set the record straight.

But if you are one of those who think that Rudy was just lucky, or as with the case involving Ronald Reagan, it was pixie dust that did it, please consider this.

When Rudy came to power in 1993 there were more than 2,500 violent incidents at the city's Rikers Island prison. What Rudy learned astonished and angered him. Hardly ever were there any consequences. Even in attacks involving serious injury or sometimes death, additional charges were seldom, if ever, laid against the cons.

The liberals who had been running things for some 50-odd years were operating under the belief that tacking on longer sentences wouldn't deter any of the crime.

The thug hugger's message was very loud and clear at Rikers. You can beat up, stab or even kill a fellow inmate and it's not likely anything will happen to you.

"That makes no sense," said Rudy, "from now on inmates at Rikers will be treated like anyone else. Commit a crime of any magnitude in any of my prisons and you will be charged, and your sentence added to the one you are already serving."

Even here in Canada the leftists always claim that getting tough on crime doesn't work. They insist that there is plenty of evidence that longer sentences are no deterrent. I'm not sure where they get those ideas since I have been unable to find a single jurisdiction where getting tough on crime has not reduced all forms of criminal activity dramatically. The best example of this is Rikers Island.

More than 2,500 violent incidents in 1993 with few, if any, consequences.

Eight years later after the cons learned that they would be charged and serve longer sentences that number dropped to—ready for this? Only 70 in 2001.

Let me run that past you again:

More than 2,500 violent incidents at Rikers in 1993.

Seventy violent incidents at Rikers in 2001.

That wasn't demographics or pixie dust that created the dramatic change in behaviour. That was fear of consequences, plain and simple.

When the cons learned that longer sentences would be tacked onto the ones they were already serving almost all the violence stopped.

Proving, beyond all doubt, that even the behaviour of hardened criminals can be changed when they know there will be consequences. Which is to say stiff penalties. When confronted with this solid evidence the leftists simply turn away and claim it never happened. But it did. Anyone can obtain the facts from the New York State Department of Justice.

But it's not just in New York that crime dropped dramatically following the implementation of very tough laws.

Here are some figures anyone can obtain from the California Department of Justice, Division of Criminal Information Service.

Proposition 184 was approved by the California State Legislature in 1994. It is the famous "three strikes and you're out" bill which essentially says that a person who commits two or more prior violent or serious offences and then commits a third felony will automatically receive 25 years to life in prison.

As you can imagine the howls of outrage from the left still reverberate up and down the Pacific coast. Just as we hear in Canada these days from the Liberals and NDP there were claims that jails would be overflowing, new prisons would have to be built and the cost would skyrocket. So-called criminal experts crawled out of the woodwork to claim it just wouldn't work. Tougher sentences don't deter crime, they claimed. Many of the experts boasted bucketloads of university degrees.

So what happened?

Well, I think you'll have to agree, it worked pretty well.

Let me provide just a few figures. The easiest to understand are those that compare the rate of various crime categories per 100,000 population. Have a look at this!

- Total crimes dropped from 3,491.5 in 1992 to 1,890.1 in 2002, a reduction of 45.9 per cent.

- Total violent crime was down from 1,103.9 in 1992 to 589.12 in 2002, a reduction of 46.6 per cent.

- Murder dropped from 12.5 in 1992 to 8.8 in 2002, a reduction of 29.2 per cent.

- Assault was down from 632.6 in 1992 to 418.1 in 2002, a reduction of 45.5 per cent.

- Rape dropped from 40.7 in 1992 to 28.8 in 2002, a reduction of 29.2 per cent.

I think you get the picture. After the first ten years of the "three strikes" legislation, crime in California fell back to levels not seen since the 1960s. The California crime rate continues to decline although not as dramatically as during those first ten years.

Here are two conservative, head-screwed-on-perfectly-straight rules you can take to the bank:

Rule #1   The incidence of crime escalates in direct proportion to the lack of consequences.

Rule #2   The more crime that goes unpunished, the more crime you will have.

If you are nodding your head in agreement at these profundities it is safe for you to continue reading.

However, if at any time thus far you have ripped pages out for poop paper in your bird cage or attempted to feed the whole thing to your dog, sorry, but it's too late. There's a new idea spinning around in your head. Your life will never be the same again.

Chapter 23

Mike the Knife

Every once in a while, to purge myself of guilt about something I've done or more likely didn't do, I punish myself by listening to CBC radio. I'm a man after all and thus should not be expected to remember such things as birthdays or anniversaries!

So I'm listening one afternoon to some self-described expert on sex and marriage explain to me everything I don't know about sex and marriage. The fact he admits he's not married and from what I can gather doesn't seem too clued in about sex, in no way disqualifies him from expert status. He is, let us not forget, a highly paid professor and thus his few years of non-experience trumps my decades of experience hands down. The long list of letters after his name says so.

"Money," he says gravely, "most marriages break up over money." He rattles off a hat full of statistics he claims prove his point. He talks a little bit about arguments concerning the raising of children but stays clear of some of the things that can really rumble a marriage, like dirty socks on the living room floor, plate-shaking snoring or passing gas under the sheets.

Like most experts it soon becomes very clear this guy is educated well beyond his intelligence but he does get me laughing because while I can't think of a single marriage that hit the rocks over money, believe it or not I do know two bust-ups over Mike Harris.

In both cases the husbands thought Mike was pretty close to the second coming, while the wives were just as convinced he was either the devil incarnate or Chainsaw Freddy without the mask. It polarized them into two separate, feuding, camps from which they viewed each other from greater and greater distances.

There's no question both marriages were on rocky ground before Harris stepped onto the stage, but he's the guy in the *ménage à trois* that finished things off for them.

I have stayed in touch with all four and here we are nearly ten years later and opinions are just as hardened as ever. They are still in their separate, although no longer feuding, camps.

Which is pretty well how the nation still views the former Premier of Ontario.

One camp is comprised almost exclusively of those with conservative convictions and thus enhanced understanding and appreciation of strong, purposeful and successful men.

The other camp, peering fuzzy headed at us from across the abyss of rainbow coloured dreams, is comprised pretty much of ragtag escapees from the school of common sense. All perky and radiant in the firm belief that all the world needs to resolve its conflicts is a really nice group hug.

The fact that Mike Harris pulled Ontario from the depths of economic despair, cut welfare rolls in half, oversaw the creation of 700,000 new jobs and restored the province to its position as the economic engine of the country is of no consequence to the "a group hug will solve it all" gang.

For them to even confront the possibility that it required a conservative to clean up a mess left by a socialist or a liberal would shake their entire belief system to the core. So, just as happened with Ronald Reagan, history is rewritten, contributions obliterated, facts doctored and lies become truth. It is, after all, the only way the left can continue to believe as they do.

Most of those on the left are driven by a very powerful ideology. It doesn't matter what works. It doesn't matter what the truth is. All that matters is that their view of the world prevails and if that requires a good deal of doctoring the truth, and dragging reputations through the muck and mire of outrageous lies, they have no problem with that.

No one is immune. In his new book *The Secret Knowledge*, Pulitzer Prize winning playwright David Mamet (*Glengarry Glen Ross*) writes about how he ran afoul of students and staff at a well-known American university while giving a lecture on dramatic structure.

"All was going well," he says, "until I suggested that the heroine of the story we were constructing be kidnapped by some Arab terrorists."

One student asked "Haven't the Arabs been picked on enough? Why did you specify Arabs as terrorists?"

To which Mamet says he responded, "I don't know, they came to mind perhaps because Arab terrorists bombed New York."

It was pretty well downhill from that point and before you knew it, a complaint had been launched against him for making "racially derogatory comments," and a concerted effort to have him banned from the campus was underway.

The fact that Mamet once declared that he is glad he is "no longer a brain-dead liberal" probably didn't help his cause much.

Mamet pulls no punches when he described the students: "They were and are children of privilege...the privilege taught, learned, and imbibed, in a 'liberal arts education' is the privilege to indict. These children have, in the main, never worked, learned to obey, command, construct, amend, or complete—to actually contribute to the society. They have learned to be shrill, and that their indictment, on the economy, on sex, on race, on the environment, though based on no experience other than hearsay, must trump any discourse, let alone opposition."

Mamet's experience is of course shared by many and is an illustration of one of the major differences between the two camps involved in what is a kind of culture war. A war between two competing world views. On one side—the conservative side—is a group of people who believe that there is a right and there is a wrong. They believe that, whether you are religious or not, the best way to avoid chaos, violence, instability and worse, is to follow a moral code that clearly defines what is acceptable and what is not, and allowing opposing views is not only acceptable but absolutely necessary.

To be a true conservative you must believe in some moral absolutes. Not all conservatives believe in all of the same absolutes, but they do agree on some very basic ones and they also know full well that there must be some absolutes. Conservatives are very firm in their belief that despite what the law may say there are some things that are just plain wrong, no ifs, ands or maybes about it.

A very good example of this is the 2006 debate in Parliament during which the age of sexual consent was raised from 14 to 16. Every true conservative in the country knew full well that telling a child that the day he or she turns 14 they can have sex with anyone of any age and there is nothing the parents can to do to stop it, is just plain wrong.

Liberals, the NDP and the Bloc fought for decades to retain the age of sexual consent at 14 years of age, despite the insistence of Conservatives that it be raised to at least 16. Only when the opposition parties decided they weren't ready to defeat the Government on this issue in 2008 did a bill raising the age to 16 finally pass in the House of Commons. Incredibly it only squeaked by with a plurality of three votes in the Liberal dominated Senate.

If you are a conservative you may be scratching your head about now and saying well of course there must be a right and a wrong in order for society to function coherently. Everybody believes that! We learned right and wrong at our mother's knee.

Ah, but you see, there you are wrong. One of the things that defines those on the left is that they believe that morality—right and wrong—is simply a personal decision. Many will tell you that right and wrong—morality—is really all relative. It depends upon the circumstances. It depends upon a person's individual point of view. I hear this all the time on my show.

"Well," callers will say, "that's all very well and good in our society, but who are we to judge other cultural norms?" When pressed, as I have been known to do, few of them have the guts to come right out and say it, but the implication is clear. They believe that if someone else's culture requires the stoning of adulterous women, we have no right to judge or condemn. In other words, stoning women to death is only wrong in some circumstances. According to them, we cannot always say stoning women, or lopping off arms, or noses, or ears is wrong. There are no absolutes in their world. And for sure we must not even suggest that some cultural practices are wrong.

That view, of course, is the very basis of multiculturalism that has as its foundation the belief that all cultures, and thus all cultural practices, are of equal value. If we oppose the stoning of women or genital mutilation it is only because we have no appreciation for others' cultural and religious beliefs. Any attempt to impose Western cultural norms on others is racism. Or so the left insists.

This whole business of much of the Arab world's obvious hatred of women poses a serious dilemma for most of those who promote multiculturalism.

Because if they admit that the oppression and violence towards women in many Middle Eastern countries are barbaric but almost un-heard of here in Canada, then they would have to admit that our cul-ture is superior to theirs. As far as the left is concerned such thinking is restricted to knuckle-dragging redneck non-progressive conserva-tives. Admit that genital mutilation is not only wrong but also com-monplace in some countries and the next thing you know you're in the George Bush camp, reading Ezra Levant and listening to Lowell Green!

That's why leading Liberal Justin Trudeau wrinkled his handsome nose and suggested that describing such practices as honour killing as barbaric made him feel uncomfortable. "Barbaric is such a pejo-rative word," he complained. The obvious implication being that burying a woman up to her neck and then throwing stones at her until she is battered to death is not barbaric. Or at the very least we should use a more polite term in public.

You have to ask yourself, why would his initial reaction be to balk at a harsh denunciation of those who hate and harm women?

John Robson, one of the leading conservative thinkers of our time says: "The problem is that they [modern liberals] are also commit-ted to a mentally and politically paralyzing cultural relativism, driven more by sentiment and snobbery than serious thought, that renders their core beliefs unredeemably incoherent."

Chapter 24

Conservative Preventive Medicine

It took Churchill, Thatcher, Reagan, Giuliani and Harris to pull their countries, provinces or cities out of the muck and mire of liberal addle-brained folly, but we've got plenty of other examples of conservative-minded administrations supplying preventive medicine.

As the world teeters on the brink of economic chaos let's just for a moment examine the jurisdictions that are doing just fine thank you very much.

Let's start with the one economy that is more or less bailing out most of the rest of Europe. That of course would be Germany, which, having had an up-close experience with extreme socialism, is today undoubtedly by far the most conservative of all nations in the European Union. Interestingly enough those in the deepest doo-doo—Greece and Spain—are by far the most socialist. In Greece, for heaven's sake, you can retire with a full government pension almost before you're out of diapers.

Then on this side of the pond we have—thank heavens—Canada, whose economy we are told is today the strongest in the G20, with the possible exception of Germany. It is no coincidence that Germany is being guided through these difficult times by the strong conservative leadership of Angela Merkel, who by the way, having obviously read my book *Mayday! Mayday!* has served notice that multiculturalism is not working in her country!

In case you hadn't noticed, Canada has had a Conservative government since well before the "recession." And let's go even further.

Please, just for the fun of it, identify the two provinces in Canada with the strongest economies today. Right! I knew you knew. Of course, Alberta and Saskatchewan. Is it just a coincidence that both of those provinces have Conservative governments?

Let's push on with our little quiz. Which province's economy rebounded the fastest and furthest when the voters finally smartened up and rescued themselves from the NDP and elected a Conservative government? Right again, Saskatchewan!

I could also ask you which two provinces were plunged into near bankruptcy by NDP governments, but reminding you that heading them were Bob Rae in Ontario and Ujjal Dosanjh in BC isn't really necessary. You already knew that and by the way, I don't need to remind you that both of those birds are now Liberals!

Now my final question. Which "have-not" province gets the biggest handout from the "have" provinces? If you said Quebec you are 100% correct. Congratulations. Now for double or nothing. Which is Canada's most socialist province? You're a winner. Quebec!

Now if you are a lefty you're going to poo-poo all of this and claim it's just coincidence that the places not teetering or tottering are all being run by conservatives. Maybe. Maybe so. But you can bet your bottom dollar that if it were the other way around, that it was conservative administrations steering us towards reefs of destruction, can you just imagine what the CBC, *The Toronto Star*, and company would be screaming today?

The bare facts stare us in the face. Those jurisdictions headed by conservative governments, real conservative governments that is, not the semi-conservative kind as in the UK, are weathering the economic storms in a relatively healthy state.

You can take another fact to the bank. The further to the left the government is, the deeper in debt they are.

Here's another prime example. No one would dispute the fact that California is the most leftist state in the Union. Is it nothing but coincidence that it went broke long before the Wall Street fiasco, and to this day remains the worst economic basket case in the US?

Does anyone else see a pattern here?

Chapter 25

Of Privilege and Morality

For the left, morality is relative. And it doesn't just have to apply to foreign cultures. How many times have you heard the claim that the criminal is actually the victim?

I recall several years ago in Ottawa, a woman walked into her boyfriend's bedroom and shot and killed him while he slept. She was let off with a couple of years of house arrest. The judge and jury bought into the argument that the boyfriend had verbally abused her and she was the real victim. She could have left him at any time; there was no evidence of physical abuse; the man was sound asleep when he was shot in the back; but no matter. The real victim here was the woman. Leftist's interpretation—the only time you can't shoot a sleeping person is if they have never yelled at you.

In the non-conservative world, murder, even of the defenseless, isn't necessarily wrong. Some even go far as to assert that the only real criminal activity is perpetrated by society. If some thug robs or kills, it's not really his fault. Society, sometimes called "the system" has failed him. He didn't get to see Bambi as a child. His mother wouldn't let him eat chocolate or he dropped out of school at age three. Whatever, it's society's fault.

This belief is typified by a letter to the editor of *The Globe and Mail*, written by David Schatzky of Toronto, and published April 11, 2011:

> *There's a growing tendency in Canada to look at someone who breaks any kind of law as a morally depraved, evil person.*
>
> *There's virtually no appreciation for the complexity of human personality, background, context, social status or mental capacity, and there's no distinction made between a one-time offender and a true criminal recidivist.*
>
> *I fear we're losing the social will to rehabilitate instead of punish.*
>
> *Revenge is not justice; the urge to throw the book at an offender and to not see criminals as victims too shows a breakdown—not only in compassion, but also in common sense.*

The letter is filled with absolute nonsense and a total lack of understanding of how our justice system works. Of course there is a distinction made by the courts between a first time offender and a recidivist. In fact most judges go overboard to ensure that a first-time offender does not go to jail, unless it is a particularly heinous crime. Our courts also take into account the mental capacity of the accused, but to suggest that somehow we are supposed to adjust sentencing according to the criminal's personality, social status or background is pure left wing hogwash. And please note Mr. Schatzky's insistence that the criminal is the victim. Also very interesting is his failure to even mention the fact that when a crime is committed there is always a *real* victim for whom very frequently there is no compassion, let alone recovery of loss.

The woman who shot and killed her sleeping boyfriend spent a couple of years living with her mother on the west coast. Her boyfriend ceased living the moment she shot him.

There are cases, sadly, of legitimate child abuse of all kinds and far too many children are being raised with very little parental supervision, but in the end it is the criminal who makes the decision to commit a crime. Fact is, most people with terrible childhoods do not become criminals.

As a matter of fact, if you listen to what the "progressives" these days claim is the proper way to raise children you could easily conclude that all of my generation and probably yours too had terrible childhoods.

I mean come on, none of us had "Dancing With the Stars" to watch on TV, we wandered about the neighbourhood unsupervised all day long, and we had to do household chores, including washing the breakfast dishes after we poured milk into our own cornflakes. Even worse, we often threw snowballs at each other, played marbles for keeps, swam in polluted water and rode our bikes without a helmet. How horrible a childhood is that? And if you really want an example of how we were neglected as children consider this. Our parents never strapped us into car seats or seat belts. It's a wonder any of us managed to stay out of jail in later life.

Many of those in the so-called liberal camp believe that efforts to adhere to and enforce behavioural rights and wrongs are simply the powerful in our society forcing their views and judgments on the "victims" of society. They do not see it as necessary to maintain the standards that have evolved through centuries of mankind's struggle for freedom and democracy.

And even when the results of failed left wing policies are obvious, such as occurred in Britain prior to the Iron Lady's leadership, in the United States prior to Ronald Reagan, in New York City prior to Rudy Giuliani and in Ontario prior to Mike Harris, those on the left simply cannot bring themselves to even consider the possibility that their view of the world, their vision, their belief in a relative morality is wrong. And worse, their philosophy not only doesn't work, it often creates great harm!

Lefty translation: the policies only failed because we don't pour enough money at the problem and just as with the Soviet Union, it was a grand idea but "we just had the wrong guy at the top."

Chapter 26

No Room in the Hospital!

Nowhere is the failure of left wing policy more evident than in Canada's health care system. You know the story. In Ontario, more than 40 per cent of provincial tax dollars now go to health care. We're told that figure will continue to soar well past 60 per cent in just a few years. The wait lists in emergency wards grow ever longer. Some hospitals are now "boasting" that they have managed to get average wait times in emergency down to only 20 hours.

More than a million and a half Canadians do not have a family doctor with little prospect of ever finding one. The more outspoken of our doctors will tell you that our hospitals are among the most dangerous places on earth. Infection rates, C. difficile…the news is filled with medical horror stories.

A report issued in April 2011 by David Dodge, former governor of the Bank of Canada and Richard Dion, former economist with the Bank of Canada says unless fundamental changes are made, health care in Canada will soon be so expensive it will be beyond the ability of our society to sustain it.

Among other things, the report says the share of GDP devoted to health care has skyrocketed by 70 per cent since 1975, from seven per cent to 12 per cent and if we keep going the way we are it will be 19 per cent of GDP within the next two decades.

The report says we've got to make some very difficult choices, including some or all of the following:

- Cut non-health care services.

- Cut health care services.

- Raise taxes and fees.

- Start charging for some medical services now provided free under our universal health care system.

- Allow more privatization.

Today about 70 per cent of all health care is delivered to Canadians through the public system, which according to the report is suffering from a "chronic spending disease."

Even as I write this, Ottawa's Queensway-Carleton Hospital, having just completed a multi-million-dollar expansion, is announcing that they're going to partially shut down operating rooms for two and a half months every year because there's not enough money to operate them. Which begs the question—why the hell did we build them in the first place?

Meantime in downtown Ottawa, one of the largest, most spectacular projects in the city's history not only has been completed on time and below budget, it is so successful we're now going to have to build more hotels to accommodate all those anxious to become frolicking conventioneers.

I refer to the magnificent new Ottawa Convention Centre, the pride and joy of the capital city.

But let's leave the new Convention Centre and head just a little bit east in Ottawa where you will find the City's brand new bus garage—built nearly a year behind schedule and about 50 million dollars over budget. And according to many drivers I have talked with, not very well-suited for the job it was designed for.

Now head south to Ottawa's relatively new privately-owned award-winning international airport, built on time and below budget.

You could carry out similar exercises in every Canadian city, town and village. Private enterprise complete the projects on time and below budget. Government projects are completed behind schedule and well over budget.

I have been unable to find comparable figures for Canada, but in the United States a study found that fully 78 per cent of government projects at all levels were over budget, behind schedule or both, compared to fewer than 32 per cent of private projects. I suspect Canadian figures are comparable.

It's not just building projects either. The cost of the long gun registry saw a "slight" increase from the forecasted $12 million to more than a billion dollars.

Then there is the infamous Ontario eHealth scam where, according to the provincial Auditor General, about one billion dollars was poured down the drain with little if anything to show for it, except of course golden handshakes for everyone who goofed up. (Sorry, make that platinum handshakes!)

I can hear you asking. What the heck is your point Green? I thought you were talking about health care!

Okay, if you haven't caught on to my point, let me spell it out. In almost every case where projects are completed on time and below budget it is private enterprise doing the job. In almost every case where the project is completed behind schedule and way over budget a government is involved. In fact, if you can point to a single government project completed on time and on budget in the past ten years in this country, I will vote Green Party in the next election.

Now I know, some of you are going to say, "Wait a minute Green, how about that watermain they repaired in Ottawa six weeks ahead of schedule in 2011?" Okay, okay, but please remember it was a private company that did the job. A private company which, by the way, was given a $430,000 bonus to speed things up and charged us close to three thousand dollars a foot to fix the thing. Let's also remember it was the city that said the job was completed six weeks ahead of schedule, which only means that's probably how long it would have taken the city to finish.

So with the evidence that surrounds us, why are we surprised that our government monopoly health care system is in shambles? How could it be otherwise? It doesn't matter which party is in power, governments, by their very nature, are horribly inefficient. There's nothing that can be done about it. It's just the way governments are and always will be.

When discussing this on my show, I often ask my listeners what they think a loaf of bread or a head of cabbage would cost if Loblaws, or any single chain, had a monopoly on providing groceries? Or what do you think an oil change would cost if only one garage in the city was allowed to do the job? What's your guess?

Remember what long distance phone calls used to cost when Bell had a monopoly?

Now let me go to the next step. What do you think a loaf of bread or a head of cabbage would cost if all groceries had to be sold through government-run stores?

I think they tried that for a while in the Soviet Union. From what I understand it didn't work so well.

But that's what we are doing with our hospitals. Leaving the supply of food to the government would be a disaster and yet that is exactly what we are doing with health care. Not only leaving it up to a monopoly, but a government monopoly. And you wonder why the entire system is in danger of coming crashing down around our ears.

Think of it. We would never entrust the supply of bread to the government, but we insist that only the government be allowed to dole out life-saving treatments and care. If we are dying, only the government is allowed to administer our deathbed needs.

Anyone over the age of four with a semi-functioning brain knows the only way we can rescue health care in this country is to allow real competition from private hospitals. Nothing will fix the problem faster at less cost than some privatization, but the Liberals, NDP and the blockheads refuse to allow us to even discuss it.

Every time there is a suggestion that we must allow more privatization of our health care system, the Liberals, NDP, Bloc and now for heaven's sake the Green Party, pull the American boogeyman out of the closet and start screaming "the sky is falling." The concept of introducing some competition for our hospitals is so frightening even some staunch Conservatives lose their way. Remember the infamous "No 2-Tier Health Care" sign that Stockwell Day flashed during the televised leaders debate for the 2000 federal election?

Only fools and those not paying attention are suggesting that Canada adopt the US style of totally private health care. Very clearly many Americans aren't exactly thrilled with what they've got, but there are many other models that combine a full public health care system with varying degrees of privatization.

Several European countries, for example, have created what they call parallel systems that work very well. With full appreciation of the fact no one should ever be denied good health care because they can't afford it, these countries have a complete publicly funded system, available to all at no cost, but there is another parallel system, either fully or partially private. In some cases patients must pay the full cost of the private system from their own pockets, or more frequently the private system is publicly funded in part.

Let's be perfectly honest here. The parallel European system I have just described is exactly what we already have in some provinces on a much smaller scale but the anti-business/anti-private enterprise sentiment is so ingrained in Canada that none of the political parties dare admit what everyone knows exists. It's the classic "the emperor has no clothes" syndrome. The left refuses to admit that private health care exists in Canada, even though not only does it stare them in the face, but also, some of the leading lights on the left actually use the private system but pretend they do not.

Nowhere is the hypocrisy and foolishness of the leftist opposition to more privatization of our health care system more apparent than the private hospital that repaired the late Jack Layton's hernia.

Chapter 27

The Shouldice Hospital

Banana Bay is a rambling, beachside restaurant on Grand Bahama Island boasting palm tree shaded rickety picnic tables, wonderful cracked conch, pigeon peas and rice. Well removed from the bustling city of Freeport, there are few places anywhere as well suited for wasting away a sunny afternoon in the company of a couple Bahama Mamas. (It's a drink!)

The owner is a tall, splendidly handsome young Italian who came to the Island as a blackjack dealer at a local casino, married the beautiful daughter of the richest man on the Island and today considers himself the luckiest guy on the planet. "Wonderful!" and a big smile are Daniel's responses to anyone who inquires after his health.

He still had the "wonderful" part going last year when we visited, but you could see he was having a tough time with the smiling. "Hernia," he said with a bit of a grimace. I suggested it was probably the weight of all the money he was lugging about which gave him a chuckle. "How far do you guys live from Toronto?" he asked. He shook his head when I told him. "Too far; I was thinking of asking if you could show me around a little bit when I'm up there for the operation."

Believe it or not, Daniel, who very clearly has more than enough money to buy himself the best surgeon in the world, was booked into the Shouldice Hospital just north of Toronto. His decision was based on advice from his doctor at one of Miami's famous private hospitals. He was told that the Shouldice Hospital was the best in the world for hernia surgery. "Its techniques," his doctor said, "are now being used in thousands of hospitals in almost every Western nation."

In fact, the Shouldice Hospital on its letterhead makes claim to being "The global leader in external abdominal wall hernia surgery for over 65 years."

Some of the other facts concerning Shouldice are fascinating. For example, the surgeons there insist that every patient remain in hospital for three days following surgery. It's to ensure there are no complications or infection. What's astounding is that Shouldice charges exactly the same fee for the operation and the three-day stay as Ontario pays for the same operation and a one-night stay or even day surgery in a regular hospital.

This pretty well shoots down the leftist argument that private hospitals, because they operate at a profit, will gouge whoever is paying.

But if Shouldice charges the same fee for a three-night stay as your local hospital charges for one night, or even day surgery, you really have to wonder who is doing the gouging.

And by the way those extra days you are staying at the Shouldice aren't spent just lying around watching television. Just listen to what the hospital has to say about those three extra days:

> *The patient-centred recovery program at Shouldice has been specially designed to promote healing in hernia patients.*
>
> *During your recovery our nurses will provide the specialized care you need to avoid any post-surgical complications. Most complications develop in the first 48 hours after surgery and a short hospital stay alleviates any concerns or anxiety for patients and their families. You will also get the rest, nutrition and exercise necessary for healthy healing.*
>
> *More importantly you'll enjoy a confident recovery with a rapid return to normal activities. You'll meet other patients who have been through the operation already and are happy to reassure you and answer your questions. Peer-to-peer mentoring is important because it relieves stress and promotes a positive attitude to recovery. We have found that this unique approach to post-operative treatment is the best way to prepare patients for a quick return to a normal lifestyle.*

But the Shouldice's global reputation is centred primarily on the expertise and special techniques that have been developed there over the years.

Here's what the hospital has to say about that:

> *At Shouldice Hospital, we set high standards. Our surgeons are fully qualified and licensed to perform surgery by the appropriate Canadian authorities. Then they are required to spend up to six months of intensive training in the Shouldice Technique to perfect their skills before they are approved to lead a Shouldice surgical team. Only surgeons practicing at Shouldice Hospital receive this training. The Shouldice Technique is very detailed and must be practiced in high volumes to ensure consistently superior results.*

> *Most general surgeons will repair 20 to 30 hernias in a year. Shouldice surgeons average over 700 cases a year which provides the highest level of practice and experience in the world. This is why Shouldice surgeons are the world's most experienced leaders in hernia repair. Surgeons come from around the globe to observe the Shouldice Technique. For two or three days, they can watch as the Shouldice repair is performed by Shouldice specialists. However, this is not training and we cannot guarantee the quality of surgery carried out by anyone other than fully qualified Shouldice surgeons.*

Pretty amazing isn't it.

Now if you are wondering why I am spending so much time talking about the Shouldice Hospital it is to illustrate something very important.

The Shouldice Hospital is a private hospital.

The Shouldice Hospital, so far as the NDP, Liberals and the Bloc are concerned should not be allowed to exist. This is a private hospital. This, according to the leftists, is the kind of thing that will destroy universal health care.

I ask again—how could anyone with his or her head screwed on straight want to close down the Shouldice Hospital? You also have to ask yourself how could a man like the late Jack Layton, whose hernia was repaired at the Shouldice, stand in front of millions of TV viewers with a straight face and claim privatization of hospitals will destroy health care in Canada?

Now there's something else about the Shouldice Hospital you should know. It's a private hospital but if you are an Ontario resident, OHIP pays the full bill for all medical procedures. Figure that one out. Every government we've ever had in Ontario including, sadly, Conservative governments, have opposed what they call two-tier health care—that is, no private health care—but they have all continued to publicly fund the Shouldice Hospital, a private hospital.

For other insured Canadians, except those from PEI, fees will be fully, or partially covered by inter-provincial insurance plans. Most private insurance plans, including those in the United States will pay for the semi-private accommodations at Shouldice.

All of which begs the question. If we not only allow the private Shouldice Hospital to operate, but publicly fund it through various provincial health insurance plans, why can't we have similar hospitals specializing in, for example, knee and hip replacements? During the 2007 election campaign, Progressive Conservative leader John Tory proposed just that, but we all know what happened to him.

But why stop with just knee and hip replacements? Why can't we have a private hospital specializing in gall bladder surgery or cataract surgery? What's so special about hernias that we allow a publicly funded private hospital for hernias but not gall bladders?

There was a dreadful front page story recently about a nine-year-old Ottawa boy denied a desperately needed gall bladder operation for more than three months because there aren't enough beds in the Children's Hospital of Eastern Ontario. His pain from gallstones has been severe enough to require daily doses of morphine and Tylenol since December 2010. Doctors say all he needs is a simple gallbladder operation but more than four months later, they still can't find him a bed and worse than that, an operation scheduled for April 14, 2011, was postponed for yet another three weeks. According to hospital officials on the day the boy's surgery was scheduled they were short 21 beds!

This is the universal publicly funded health care system that works so well we must not even discuss an alternative?!

So I ask all of our political leaders and all the leftists who refuse to even discuss private hospitals or clinics, what in the world would be wrong with a private hospital performing gallbladder removals as skillfully and as cost-effectively as the Shouldice Hospital repairs hernias? And if your concern is that it is only "rich" people who can afford preferred medical treatment, and that shouldn't be allowed, then, just as with the Shouldice Hospital, provide public funding so no one is denied. Can anyone tell me how publicly funded, private "centres of excellence" would damage Canada's health care system, let alone destroy it?

And while we are at it, why not allow private MRI and/or CT scan clinics? When Liberal Premier Dalton McGuinty came to power in 2003, Ontario had several private MRI clinics that operated very effectively and helped to shorten the long lineups at our hospitals. One of the first things McGuinty did was take $25 million tax dollars and buy out the private clinics, either shutting them down or converting them to public facilities. The result was ever-longer wait times and much higher costs.

Did this improve health care? Of course not. So why did he do it? The answer boils down to one thing: Socialist ideology, pure and simple. The same socialist ideology that sentences a nine-year-old boy to more than four months of agonizing pain and, increasingly, is rationing health care so drastically that lives are now at risk.

About three years ago, a spinal injury became serious enough that doctors feared without immediate surgery I might lose the use of my right leg. I desperately needed an MRI to determine the extent of the injury and the exact location. The wait time for the MRI, I was told, was about six months.

Unwilling to have me risk partial paralysis, my wife picked up the phone and booked an appointment for the very next day at a private clinic just across the Ottawa River in Gatineau, Quebec. The clinic was modern, efficient, very professional, friendly and fast. Not only did they have a full MRI scan for my doctor within 24 hours but they also presented me with a neat jacket, which I still wear.

The cost with taxes was a bit under $800. Not cheap by any means, but considering the alternative, a wonderful bargain. The money sadly came right out of my pocket since OHIP refuses to cover the cost. I can't even use it as a medical expense on my income tax form. It's a private clinic, you see. I must be punished for using it. What the leftists claim is that I should have endured incredible pain for six months and risked losing the use of a leg, because using the private clinic is somehow promoting two-tier health care that will, along with global warming and Stephen Harper, destroy the planet! All to satisfy socialist ideology.

You've got to understand it is perfectly acceptable for leading politicians to have their hernias repaired at a private hospital, but if you or I need an MRI or CT scan—even to save our lives—well, you'll just have to get in line for a few months. And if you or I dare take money from our own pockets for a private clinic, we must be punished.

Even more bizarre than any of this was the reaction of some of my callers when I told them what I had done.

"You jumped the queue. Most people can't afford $800; you rich people are all the same, you all get special privileges; it's guys like you who are going to destroy our health care system; two-tier health care shouldn't be allowed; you should wait your turn like everyone else," were a few typical comments.

"Jumped the queue?" I said to one bozo. "Jumped the queue? What the hell are you talking about? I didn't jump the queue. I got out of the queue and let someone else in. I took money out of my own pocket and everyone who was in the queue moved up one space. You should be thanking me!"

The whole thing sure makes you wonder whether the problem may not be that we've got far too many people whose heads aren't screwed on straight, but rather they haven't got their heads screwed on at all!

By the way, just to follow up. Our Bahamian friend Daniel spent a day at the Shouldice Hospital early in 2011. A team of their experts examined him and concluded that he did not require surgery for a hernia.

Chapter 28

The Thought Police

Remember the scene that went viral on YouTube when the Alberta Human Rights Commissioner, Shirlene McGovern, while grilling Ezra Levant on charges of expressing an opinion, flabbergasted us all by claiming: "You're entitled to your opinions." To which Mr. Levant responded: "I wish that were a fact!"

Here was Ezra, dragged into a kangaroo court, denied a lawyer, not allowed to face his accuser, charged with not only having an opinion but actually stating it by publishing the Mohammed cartoons that had ignited riots in much of the Arab world, being told by his interrogator that he was entitled to the opinion he was charged with expressing. Talk about *Alice in Wonderland*!

That was bizarre enough, but the thing that enraged Ezra and many of the rest of us was when he was asked what his *thoughts* were when he had the cartoons published.

There it was front and centre for all to see and marvel at. The thought police in action. The Alberta Human Rights Commission was demanding to know what Ezra Levant's thoughts were because, incredibly, Human Rights Commissions across the land have, as part of their mandate, the right to access and punish you for your thoughts. "What were your thoughts when you decided to publish the cartoons?" Ezra was asked. The implication was very clear that if Ezra was thinking that publishing the cartoons would embarrass or humiliate Muslims his actions were more sinful and thus more punishable than if he just did it as some kind of lark. The degree of punishment thus would be directly related to his thoughts.

Shocking when you stop to think about it.

But let's understand something here. The thought police are hard at work everywhere in our criminal justice system.

Hate crime legislation creates crimes out of thoughts.

Let me explain. If you beat up a man because you don't like something he said, or you don't like his politics, or you think he's ugly, that's just good old-fashioned assault or a similar charge. But, if you beat up that same guy because you don't like the colour of his skin, or his sexual preference, that's a hate crime and the punishment is more severe.

Punch a guy who makes a pass at your girlfriend, take out half of his teeth, break his nose and open him up for 50 stitches and you will likely receive a lighter sentence than if you only slightly bruise someone because he's black or a homosexual. That's because the crime then becomes not the assault itself, but your reason for doing it. In other words, your thoughts.

It's a difficult concept to grasp so let me give you another illustration. Suppose you punch a homosexual, or a black man or a Muslim or a Jew. Is it a hate crime and thus subject to a much stiffer sentence than would otherwise be the case? It all depends upon what you were thinking when you threw the punch. Was it because the guy insulted you or was it because of his colour, sexual preference or religion? What your thoughts were when you threw the punch becomes the determining factor. Thus it is that under our hate laws, the act may still be a crime, but your thoughts when committing the act constitute an additional crime and, incredibly, you will be punished for your thoughts.

Hate crime legislation pertaining to many different groups was passed by former Liberal governments, and a 2004 amendment added sexual preference to the list of protected groups at the urging of the NDP, but I cannot absolve the Progressive Conservatives. The government of Brian Mulroney had a chance to scrap, or at the very least modify, hate legislation but chose not to deal with it.

There was no way any changes to the legislation could have been made by a minority Conservative government under Stephen Harper, but times have changed. There are other, more pressing matters Harper's new majority government must deal with, but at the urging of Conservatives across the country let's hope the new Parliament bucks up the courage to scrap any legislation making your thoughts a crime. Because, let's face it, creating a crime out of your thoughts is a tyrannical left wing concept that no true conservative would ever agree to.

What we're dealing with when it comes to hate, or thought crimes, is political correctness carried to extreme. American political commentator Rush Limbaugh has an interesting suggestion in this regard when he says: "For all intents and purposes, political correctness is now an absolute term. It is far too polite and genteel a label to describe the brand of political oppression being imposed on certain kinds of thought. From now on, let's call it what it is—thought control and political cleansing.

"Why do I call it political cleansing?" asks Limbaugh, "Because when the Serbs launched a genocidal scorched earth policy against the Muslim population in Bosnia it was characterized as ethnic cleansing. Liberals are up to the same thing—only instead of wiping out a people, they are targeting certain ideas and viewpoints."

He goes on to say, "Liberals so monopolize the marketplace of opinion because of their domination of the media, the arts and the schools, that some of them have come to believe that their pet theories and beloved philosophical constructs have no legitimate intellectual competition so they just declare other viewpoints off limits. That's what I mean by political cleansing. The hypocrisy of it is palpable. The left-wing thought police are forever paying lip service to the ideals of free expression, but they are the first ones in line to place restrictions on it for those with whom they disagree."

What we are dealing with, both in the United States where hate crime laws are also being imposed, and here in Canada, is vintage liberalism. It is the left that has concocted the bizarre idea that we can determine the severity of the crime on the basis of why the crime was committed. We have always graded offences based on the perpetrator's state of mind or intent. Kill someone unintentionally and you will be punished far less severely than if you intended to do to it and planned the act in advance. But never, before the introduction of the hate crime concept, have our courts been instructed to grade criminal offences and their punishment on why a person committed the crime, except in the case of forethought, which applied no matter who you killed.

There is no question bigotry is bad. It is repugnant and completely stupid, but until the passage of hate crime legislation those feelings, those thoughts, were not a crime. Now we have made it a crime to not only express those thoughts, but in some cases even to hold them. In fact we have made it a crime to hold hateful thoughts. (Please keep this in mind the next time some bozo cuts you off in traffic. Your thoughts may be illegal.)

Well actually that statement is not entirely true. Not all crimes carried out because of hate fall under hate crime legislation. For example, if you kill your husband because you hate him it is not a hate crime. If you can convince the jury or the judge that he was abusive you may not even have to spend a day in jail. It's only natural that you hate the drunk driver who killed your daughter, but if you kill the drunk in a fit of rage it is not a hate crime. Not long ago a woman pulled a gun in a New York courtroom and shot the man accused of molesting her son. "I hate you!" she screamed as she pulled the trigger. She was not charged with a hate crime.

I could go on and provide hundreds of similar examples of how murders and lesser crimes have been committed out of pure hatred, but hate crime charges were not laid.

Here is the truth of the matter. The left in this country really doesn't care if a crime is committed out of hatred, unless the hatred is of a politically incorrect variety. Shoot someone because you hate the individual and it is not a hate crime. Shoot someone because you dislike the fact that the individual is part of a specific group (race, national or ethnic origin, language, colour, religion, sex, age, mental or physical disability, sexual orientation, or any other similar factor) and you will likely be charged with a hate crime.

Now let me raise another question here.

If our government can make it a crime to be a racist or a bigot, why not criminalize other viewpoints. The left claims that creating a hate crime is not an infringement of free expression because the thought is coupled with a criminal act and it is the act that is being punished. But that argument doesn't hold water, because in the case of hate crimes, yes the act is punished, but so is the thought itself that accompanies the act. In Canada the thought can get you an extra five years in jail.

As Rush Limbaugh and others point out, this is the insidious way the thought police can get their feet in the door to impose the tyranny of their views on the rest of society through the awesome enforcement authority of the criminal justice system. How long will it be before governments decide to make it illegal to oppose green energy initiatives or excess bovine flatulence? These issues, just as with racism, prompt people to take strong political and moral positions. After all, what's unique about racist or bigoted viewpoints? Why should they be the only immoral positions to be criminalized?

In fact, in Canada we already have some laws that come very close to making it illegal to take positions opposed to abortion. In fact, as Ezra Levant learned to his great consternation, we now have laws administered through the various human rights commissions that can make a criminal out of you for publishing cartoons. And a worse criminal depending upon your thoughts.

I'd like to hear what you think about thought crimes and the thought police. As far as I can determine it's still legal to talk about it!

Chapter 29

You Owe Me

A 53-year-old unemployed woman from Sainte-Angèle-de-Prémont, Quebec, named Muguette Paillé became a big star following the French Language debate held during the 2011 Federal Election campaign when she asked what the government was going to do to find her a job.

Within hours, six Facebook sites were established in her name and "Mme Paillé" became one of Twitter's top ten most mentioned words in Canada.

Very clearly half the country thinks the government should find her a job. The other half, the conservative half with their heads screwed on straight, believes Muguette should find her own job or create one! The last thing in the world conservatives want is any more of the nanny state being shoved down our throats. Most of us are only too aware that the most frightening seven words in the English language are: "The government is here to help you."

Let me give you another example of how more and more people are coming to the belief that the government is there to look after us from cradle to grave.

An angry young Green Party supporter called me on the show a few days prior to the May 2, 2011, federal election with the intent of giving me a good solid public flogging. She was mad as hell because many of my callers were opposed to taxpayers having to fund political parties through vote subsidies.

"Why should they take money from me to give to the Green Party?" I asked her, "and how about the Bloc Québécois? Why should any of my tax money go to them?" I pointed out that in 2010, the Bloc took four dollars from Canadian taxpayers for every dollar that was voluntarily donated to them.

She wasn't buying any of it. "Making taxpayers fund political parties is all about democracy," she insisted. "Mr. Green, you've got lots of money to support a political party, but I'm a student, I don't have any money." I suggested she could cut back on a couple week's worth of beer purchases and kick in five bucks to the Green Party, but she became quite indignant, claiming, "I don't drink beer!" I forgot to ask her about single malt scotch, but that's another story.

"Well," I said, "look, if you don't have any money to help out your party why don't you volunteer? You can do a bit of work for them."

This seemed to puzzle her to no end. "What do you mean?"

"Bang in a few lawn signs, make a few phone calls, knock on some doors. Look, you want the government to take money out of my pocket to help fund the Greens, if you don't have any money, then volunteer your services for them."

There was a pause. Then, in a shocked voice, "Do you mean for free?!"

I couldn't believe it. Here was this young, obviously very bright woman adamant that tax money should be taken from us all to support her party of choice, but sadly she has a brain so obviously warped by leftist ideology that the idea that she should have to contribute anything shocked her.

Her message was loud and clear. Not only does someone owe me an education but you've also got to support the political party I choose, and I don't have to lift a finger. Isn't that a lovely piece of work?

Stay tuned folks. It's the nanny state in full bloom! But as the saying goes, "You ain't seen nothin' yet." Just wait until we get government-run potty training!

Having people like Muguette Paillé step up to the microphone and demand to know what the government is going to do for them is something liberals and socialists absolutely love. They claim it's because they are the compassionate ones, but in fact liberalism and socialism owe their very existence to the dependency of others. The more people who become dependent upon government for more things, the more liberalism and socialism are likely to blossom. The last thing liberals and socialists want is a hard working, self-reliant society.

When I so foolishly campaigned on behalf of the Liberal Party in 1983 in Ottawa Centre I was astonished at the number of people demanding favours of me, even though I was only an unelected candidate. More than one suggested they might vote for me if I could persuade their landlord to lower the rent. One lovely woman took me into her backyard and absolutely insisted that I speak to her next-door neighbour about a tree whose shadow she claimed was killing her raspberry plants. I can't begin to tell you the number of people who demanded that I find a job for them or a relative.

I vividly recall the young woman who asked if I knew anyone hiring social workers. I suggested she call Big Brothers, which I knew had just lost an employee. The very next day she called back to flay the hide off my back for sending her on what she claimed was a wild goose chase. They had already hired someone and it was all my fault.

I was not the least bit surprised when voters in the riding voted heavily in favour of the socialist/NDP candidate, and as a matter of fact that's still the way they vote in that riding most of the time. Very clearly the majority of the voters in Ottawa Centre have lost so much faith in themselves that they have come to believe only the government can solve their problems, and as in the case with Muguette Paillé, find a job for them.

Even more discouraging is the fact that most of the media seem to think Mme Paillé was the hero of the day.

Liberals and socialists will huff and puff at this suggestion, but I firmly believe we've got to work a lot harder at convincing people that the government cannot solve any of the country's social problems. If governments could, there would be no unemployment in Canada, no poverty, no crime, and no homelessness. But the fact is, governments cannot put a chicken (or maybe a Canada goose) in every pot. Good governments can create a climate that promotes employment, but our citizens must understand that it is they who must venture out from the government safety net to find those jobs and when they do, work hard to retain them.

It may sound simplistic, but the fact remains that we must once again begin to teach self-reliance in this country. We need to re-establish the kind of work ethic that built Canada in the first place. (I know, I know, I'm dreaming in Technicolor, but just because I'm conservative doesn't mean that I can't dream a bit. Heck, some conservatives I know even like ballet and opera!).

By now, surely, we must all understand that when people are given something for nothing they do not value it as highly as if they had gone out and earned that something through their own efforts. We should also have learned that government handouts, with no strings attached, ultimately rob individuals and, for that matter, entire communities of their dignity and pride.

I will never forget the social worker who called me from Toronto to boast that she advised all of her unemployed clients not to take minimum wage jobs. "I tell them," she said, "that employers paying minimum wages are just exploiters getting rich on the backs of the young, the poor and the uneducated." She was obviously very proud of the advice she was handing out and assured me that, in fact, she had persuaded many people to stay on welfare rather than take a poorly paid job."

"What about the dignity of work?" I asked. She didn't understand. "Do you really tell your clients there is more dignity in taking welfare than in taking a low paid job?" Her response was emphatic, "Of course! And I'm certainly not the only one handing out that advice."

The conversation went on for some time. I tried to point out that most low paid jobs are starter jobs, a good place to begin climbing the employment ladder. I also pointed out that when her clients are later looking for a better job, most employers would have great respect for someone who turned down welfare in favour of work, no matter how poorly paid.

She wasn't buying any of it. As far as she was concerned, and she assured me most of her fellow social workers in Toronto believed the same thing, her clients, no matter what their education, skill level, work experience or work ethic deserved a highly paid job and if it wasn't handed to them on a platter then the government damn well owed them a good living, and by the way, "welfare payments should be a lot higher," she claimed.

Very clearly she was absolutely convinced that her client's inability to obtain a "dream job" was entirely society's fault with no responsibility falling upon the client's shoulders.

When I suggested she was doing a great disservice to the people she advised and pointed out that it was in her own best interest to keep as many people on welfare as possible she became very angry, accusing me of some pretty unsavoury things.

I finally hung up in abject disgust.

What she, and I fear many others on the left are doing is creating a parasitic class. A subculture of people, who, while fully capable of producing and creating a good life for themselves, are instead wallowing in self-pity, assured by social workers and others on the left that they are helpless victims and virtually powerless against the terrible forces of capitalism.

What all of this requires, of course, is ever-larger governments who take ever-larger chunks of tax money from those of us who do work, produce, save and take risks. The money thus confiscated from us is handed over to those who are not productive.

To be totally accurate a good chunk of the money they take from us never makes it to my caller's clients or to anyone who really needs and deserves it. Much of the money they take from us supposedly to assist those who cannot help themselves remains stuck in the pockets of the ever-larger bureaucracy required to administer all of this "goodwill."

Ever-higher taxes and other forms of fees (eco taxes, health taxes, sewage fees, and so on) almost inevitably shrink the productive sector of our society, thus spreading the misery around. Spreading the misery around, don't forget, according to liberals and socialists, is compassion and fairness.

I will say it again: By promising more and more government help we are doing all Canadians a great disservice. Convincing people to rely more and more on government and less and less on themselves is the worst thing any government can do. This is not compassion. It is in fact a form of exploitation. To tell people that they have no control over their own destiny is destructive and cruel.

Today, more than ever, Canada's economic recovery requires less government and more entrepreneurial spirit. We need more hard workers, more productivity, more risk-taking and, yes, the profits that fund more and more opportunity.

Government handouts only discourage that which is most desperately needed—self-reliance, pride and confidence in our country and ourselves. A few more people with their heads screwed on straight would help as well. Governments can provide none of that, but they can certainly discourage it.

Far too many Canadians live in poverty today because they have been conditioned to depend upon someone else for their prosperity. They have been told time and time again that there is nothing they can do for themselves; nothing they can do to improve their lot in life, but instead must depend on others, in most cases, big government, to do everything for them.

Conservatives, on the other hand believe that the great majority of people in this country are quite capable of looking after themselves and make a decent living for their families. We conservatives have great faith in the individual human spirit. We have studied and understand very well the tremendous handicaps our forefathers overcame to present to us this grand land. Many of us have overcome tremendous obstacles ourselves in order to achieve success.

Very few conservatives were born with a silver spoon in their mouths. We know that hard work will overcome many of the handicaps we may have been born with. I remember my father telling me that those of us who know how to work hard and are prepared to do so, already have a great leap up in life.

Thank heavens, Canada is a country where there is room for everyone to find success, but that success will not come if you believe the leftist message that you don't stand a chance, that the deck is stacked against you and that there is no sense in even trying.

What conservatives believe and preach is that we should all strive to be the very best that we can be and if we fail, all it means is we've got to pick ourselves up, dust ourselves off and start all over again.

If you haven't hit the canvas a few times in your life, all it means is you just aren't trying hard enough.

Chapter 30

Of Eggs and Prayer

S o the question goes like this: When is an egg not an egg? Answer: When it's an Easter egg. Why? Well you'll have to ask the lefty eggheads in Seattle, Washington, because they are the only ones who can explain it.

Believe it or not, public schools in Seattle have been instructed that they cannot use the phrase "Easter egg" in classrooms. Henceforth they are to be called spring spheres. Honest! I could not make this kind of nonsense up!

In Canada, Christmas trees are rapidly being replaced by holiday trees. Both Christmas and Easter have been pretty well banished from public schools coast to coast. Oh, they still take a couple weeks off around December 25 and school is out on the day we conservatives still call Good Friday but any public recognition of the religious nature of either of these events is deemed to be offensive to the "progressives" in our midst and thus, at their insistence, must be banned.

God is dangerous don't you know?

In Saguenay, Quebec, a group of these "progressives" has served Mayor Jean Tremblay with a letter from the Quebec Human Rights Tribunal demanding that he obey a court order and immediately stop reciting a prayer at the opening of council meetings. The February 2011 letter ordered Mayor Tremblay and his council to pay an atheist $30,000 in damages after he complained about a brief prayer recited at the start of a council meeting he attended. The letter also ordered the removal of a crucifix and statue of the Sacred Heart from the council rooms. The mayor, meantime, has collected more than $180,000 in donations from local people so he can appeal the ruling in the Quebec Court of Appeal. Until then any reference to religion is banned.

In California the public school system introduced a new course called "Sex Respect." Introduced during the Ronald Reagan years, it is federally funded and stresses abstinence and the problems that often accompany premarital sex. The results were very positive. For the first time in two decades, teen pregnancies began to decline. But, once again, the "progressives" moved in with their demand that anything they do not agree with should be banned.

The American Civil Liberties Union challenged all such programs on constitutional grounds. Their lawyers claim that abstinence and marital fidelity are religious concepts and therefore inappropriate to be taught in the public school system. In Modesto, California, the left wing organization Planned Parenthood went so far as to claim that teaching abstinence is tantamount to spreading fear. The course was finally banned.

For years there have been demands that I be taken off the air. Boycotts of businesses advertising on my show have been organized. One of the campaigns that lasted more than two years was called simply "Ban Green." It has cost me a good deal of money. It has cost my employer a good deal of money. The left very clearly is prepared to go to great lengths in order to stifle views with which they do not agree.

Not too many conservatives were involved in that campaign. How many conservatives do you suppose were in that gang that forced the cancellation of Ann Coulter's address to students at the University of Ottawa?

Liberals and socialists, as you know, support all forms of free speech—as long as liberals and socialists agree with the topic. "Ban Coulter!" shouted the mob at the University of Ottawa. "She'll say things we don't agree with." Well actually they didn't come right out and say exactly that, but very clearly that's what they meant. As far as I know they didn't suggest she should be jailed for what she might say, although come to think of it, one of the head honchos at the university kind of hinted at that in an advance warning.

Has anyone on the left ever been banned from speaking at a university? You've got to be kidding! Only conservative voices must be banned! Ms. Coulter may be a nutcase, but like it or not, she has the same right to free speech as Gore/Suzuki.

The move to have Sun News Network banned was launched long before it hit the airwaves. Thousands, including some of Canada's leading journalists and intellectuals, (Margaret Atwood for one) signed a petition demanding that "Fox News North," as they branded it, not be allowed to broadcast in Canada. Ban it, they demanded, and they almost accomplished just that.

Ban this, ban that, ban anything and everything the left doesn't agree with. If the "progressives" had their way big-C and small-C conservatives, starting with Stephen Harper, would be banned and I would be right behind him, along with Ezra Levant. By no means would we be the only ones silenced. Remember how that great "progressive" David Suzuki once told university students that any opposition to the theory of global warming should be banned. He even went so far as to suggest that global warming deniers should be tossed into jail. Now that's some really "progressive" banning.

I hope you notice that both big- and small-C conservatives aren't demanding that anything be banned. Toronto Mayor Rob Ford ran into all sorts of flak when he decided to bask in cottage sunshine rather than attend the Gay Pride Parade, but he never suggested the parade be banned even though if you or I paraded around like they do in the parade, they'd toss our sorry butts into jail.

No, the "banning parade" all starts from the left. Sure there are lots of things conservatives don't like but with the enhanced wisdom and tolerance that is the mark of all true conservatives we believe in "live and let live." Not only that, but unlike the "ban gang," conservatives have discovered on/off switches, buttons and other assorted doohickeys on our radios and televisions. When a broadcaster says something we don't agree with we'll phone in to present a powerful argument or if the guy is too stupid to understand reason we simply turn him off.

If conservatives don't want to hear a prayer at a council meeting we just plug our ears for a couple of minutes. No big deal. And if Muslims, Jews and other religions want some observance of their religion in our schools, sure why not, do the kids good to see how the rest of the world lives, so long of course as we Christians are allowed to have our Christmas and Easter.

A caller from Renfrew, Ontario put it best when he told me: "Lowell, I hate snowmobiles. They are noisy and smelly and whip around too fast. But I'm a conservative, so if I don't like snowmobiles I don't buy one; I don't go around demanding that the government ban them."

His call prompted a Toronto listener to send me the following little bit of wit and wisdom. If you're still wondering which side of the political fence you sit on, here is another great test.

If a Conservative doesn't like guns, he doesn't buy one.

If a Liberal doesn't like guns he demands that the government ban them.

If a Conservative is a vegetarian, he doesn't eat meat.

If a Liberal is a vegetarian he demands that the government ban all meat products.

If a Conservative is a homosexual, he quietly leads his life.

If a Liberal is a homosexual he demands the government legislate respect.

If a Conservative is down and out, he thinks about how to better himself and looks for a job.

A Liberal demands that the government look after him and blames the government for his problems.

If a Conservative doesn't like a talk show host, he switches him off.

Liberals demand that the government ban him and all talk shows that they don't agree with.

If a Conservative doesn't agree with male circumcision he doesn't have his sons circumcised.

If a Liberal doesn't agree with male circumcision he tries to get it banned for everyone, as they are demanding in San Francisco.

If a Conservative is a non-believer, he doesn't go to church.

A Liberal non-believer demands that the government ban all religious displays and observances in the country.

If a Conservative reads this, he'll forward it to his friends so they can all have a good laugh.

A Liberal will be horribly offended and demand the government ban this kind of insult!

Let's be very honest here. It is the left, the so-called progressives who have outlawed Christmas and Easter in our public institutions; they are the ones insisting that an Easter egg be called a spring sphere.

It is the left that is suing a Quebec town over the recital of a short prayer. It is the left that banned the teaching of abstinence for teens. It is the left that demands that I be booted off the air just as it is the left including, shamefully, journalists, who tried to get Sun TV banned before it ever got started. It is the left that insists that Quebec kids in daycare must not be taught anything about any kind of religion. The left insists that if a child learns about Noah and the Ark, David and Goliath, Solomon and his wisdom they will be irrevocably damaged.

It was the left that shouted down Ann Coulter, just as it was the left that rioted and forced the cancellation of an address by former Israeli Prime Minister Benjamin Netanyahu at Montreal's Concordia University and it is the left that supports the "hatefest" called Israel Apartheid Week on many Canadian university campuses.

Don't get me wrong, there are plenty of things we conservatives don't like. We can complain, bitch, whine and wheedle with the best of them, but when it comes to demanding that things be banned the so-called progressive left are the hands-down champions.

If you have any doubt about anything I have said to this point ask yourself this question: Would any conservative insist that an Easter egg be called a spring sphere? Come on. You just know something that bizarre could only spring from a bona fide lefty brain!

Hell's bells, the eggheads who came up with that one either have never seen an egg or don't know the proper definition of a sphere. I Googled it and up popped the answer on a site called "Ask Kids." Here's what it says: "A sphere is a perfectly round, three dimensional object like a baseball or orange."

Now, I've raised a lot of chickens in my time. My father at one point counted 26 different breeds of chickens scratching and clucking around his barnyard and sometimes up onto his front porch. Some laid brown eggs, some laid white eggs, a few laid blue eggs, some eggs were mottled, some were big, some were tiny, most had only one yoke, a few had two and I once saw an egg with three yokes. Some chickens hid their eggs, others plopped them out almost underfoot.

But as God is my witness I have never ever seen a perfectly round egg. Goat poop is a sphere, yes, so are deer droppings and bowling balls, but if you ask a conservative what shape an egg is, he would look at it for a moment—turn it around and respond very correctly: "Eggs are—well—eggs are egg-shaped, any damn fool can see that!"

And if asked, will assure you that eggs do not change their shape at Easter—not even for liberals!

Chapter 31

Shooting Galleries

You would be hard-pressed to find an issue that more clearly separates liberal/socialist thinking from that of the common sense that conservatives possess, than the existence of so-called safe injection sites. In Vancouver the location on East Hastings is called InSite.

In a nutshell, liberals/socialists want so-called safe injection sites in every major Canadian city while conservatives, led by the Conservative Government, want the ones now operating shut down. Let's get something straight here please. While the "progressives" want these shooting galleries in every city, town and village on the planet there is just one proviso. They've got to be located next door to you, not them.

Vancouver, which has North America's worst drug problem, and Montreal, now boast they are the only places in North America where a drug addict can walk in with his favourite brand of hard drug and shoot it into his or her body, sometimes even with the assistance of a medical professional.

The question of whether these so-called safe injection sites are legal under our constitution and whether the BC or the federal government has jurisdiction went to the Supreme Court of Canada for a decision on May 12, 2011.

If the Court rules that shutting down the InSite location in Vancouver would violate the human rights of drug users, and the provinces have jurisdiction rather than the federal government, you can rest assured that the leftists will have these things shoved down our throats on street corners everywhere whether those of us with our heads screwed on straight want them or not.

If, on the other hand, the Court rules that the Federal Government does have jurisdiction and shutting them down is constitutional, you can bet your bottom dollar that the same kind of propaganda machine that got herbicides banned in Ontario will be unleashed on us poor beleaguered taxpayers. The leftists never rest until they have imposed their view of the world on us all.

And yes, just in case you are wondering, one of the defences being advanced in favour of InSite is that to close it would violate the human rights of drug users. Go figure!

The Federal Government's position on the matter is very clear. Drugs and drug possession are illegal and should not be condoned, be it through safe injection sites or any other way. Prime Minister Stephen

Harper has been quoted as declaring, "We as a government will not fund drug use."

But arrayed against that declaration are the reams of documents, studies, assertions, claims, promises, statistics, warnings, dire threats, pleadings and court challenges that only a well financed liberal/socialist campaign can spring on us. The kind of campaign where past experience, common sense and facts are totally abandoned.

InSite in Vancouver was the first place in North America where drug addicts can bring their drug of choice to a location and legally inject the poison into their veins with some kind of medical supervision.

It is essentially what many describe as a "shooting gallery." The addict buys the drugs on the street, brings them to InSite, obtains a free clean needle and then shoots up. There is no attempt on behalf of InSite to determine the quality of the drug or what it has been mixed with. According to officials, in 2009 InSite recorded 276,178 visits by 5,447 different addicts. The claim is that during that year 484 overdoes occurred but with no fatalities due to intervention by medical staff.

Very clearly this is a medical staff that either makes no attempt to control the amount or quality of drug being injected or very frequently is unsuccessful at such control.

A federal government study indicates that only about five per cent of Vancouver's drug addicts are served by InSite, which means that, incredibly, if the figures are correct, there are more than 100,000 drug addicts in the greater Vancouver area. Some might suggest that whatever efforts are being made to reduce the addict population aren't overwhelmingly successful.

Not only that, but a study conducted by the BC government showed that since InSite opened there has been an increase in drug-induced deaths every year. One of the InSite lobby groups claimed that this study did not deal with deaths from drug overdoses, but a careful examination of the Government study very clearly states that the deaths referred to were all from drug overdoses.

What the supporters of so-called safe injection sites don't want you to know is that at least two dozen major European cities have experimented with safe injection sites, but in 1994 the European Union signed a declaration opposing them and calling for them all to be prohibited because of the problems they created.

More recently, the city of Amsterdam has begun to shut down not only a good portion of its famous Red Light District, but many of the "coffee houses" serving up so-called soft drugs like marijuana are now off limits to tourists.

When in Holland recently, I inquired about this and was informed that organized crime had moved into both the prostitution and drug industry and that, coupled with the social problems created in the neighbourhood through the influx of sex and drug tourism, were creating so many problems government officials would like to shut it all down. Speculation is that will likely happen throughout Holland in the next few years.

Rock and roll is one thing, but very clearly sex and drugs aren't quite as "progressive" as the left would have us believe.

Here in Canada it's a very complicated issue involving both the former Chrétien Liberal Government and the current government under Stephen Harper.

In order for you to have a better understanding of the political machinations that have been underway for nearly a decade, here's a *Coles Notes* sketch of proceedings up until the time this book was published.

September 2003—InSite is launched on East Hastings Street in downtown Vancouver as a three-year pilot project. It operates under a special exemption to Section 56 of the Controlled Drugs and Substances Act. An exemption granted by the Liberal Government of Jean Chrétien.

September 2006—Federal Health Minister Tony Clement grants a 15-month extension of the project.

August 2007—Two InSite drug users file suit with the BC Supreme Court to keep the injection site open permanently. They argue that to close the site would deprive them of their rights under our Charter of Rights and Freedoms.

October 4, 2007—The Conservative Government announces a $64 million "drug strategy" to combat drug use and announces that InSite will be allowed to remain open until June 30, 2008.

March 2008—The BC Supreme Court begins to hear the InSite case.

May 2008—The BC Court rules that shutting down InSite violates the Charter and grants InSite a constitutional exemption from Federal drug laws.

A few days later—The Federal Government announces it will appeal the decision.

January 2010—The BC Court of Appeal in a two-to-one decision dismisses the Federal appeal and finds that InSite is a health care facility and thus under provincial, not federal, jurisdiction.

February 2010—The Federal Government appeals the BC decision to the Supreme Court of Canada.

May 12, 2011—The Supreme Court of Canada begins to hear the case.

What's interesting is that for the most part the same arguments are now being advanced in favour of "safe injection sites" that were used to convince Vancouver, Toronto, Ottawa and Montreal that free needles (NEP) for drug addicts would greatly improve public health.

And for the most part it is the same people now lobbying for more shooting galleries who overwhelmed and conned municipal and provincial governments into approving needle exchange programs using a tidal wave of arguments, studies, surveys, experts' opinions and outright junk science.

The experts, the medical officers of health, the university professors, the researchers, the socialists, the Marxists, the anarchists and their acolytes absolutely guaranteed us that the needle exchange programs (NEP) would greatly lessen the rates of hepatitis C (HepC) and HIV infection. We now know they barefaced lied to us; there is really no other way of describing what has happened.

Let's start with Vancouver, which when it launched its NEP in 1988 reported that about 10 per cent of injection drug users were HIV positive. A Canadian Press report five years later, December 26, 2003, stated that it was now believed fully 30 per cent of intravenous drug users were HIV positive and believe it or not 90 per cent of the users have HepC. This is while Vancouver was distributing two million free needles each year. (The figure is about three million today. Obviously the needle trade is a burgeoning industry.)

In other words, only five years after Vancouver's NEP was launched in order to lower HIV infection rates, the rate tripled. This, they claim, is such a great success the program should be expanded.

Today, while distributing more free needles than any other jurisdiction in the world, Vancouver boasts the worst HIV and HepC infection rates in the world. Ottawa's HIV and HepC infection rates are described by the city's Medical Officer of Health as a problem of "epidemic" proportions, so describing Vancouver's situation as a super-epidemic would hardly be a stretch.

Following several studies in Montreal and Vancouver, the *American Journal of Epidemiology* reported that, "NEEDLE EXCHANGE PROGRAMS DO NOT WORK." The story went on to say, "Vancouver's HIV infection rate among injection drug users who use NEP is higher than drug users who do not take part in the program. Furthermore," states the Journal, "the Vancouver findings are similar to those throughout the world. Montreal addicts in the NEP recorded an HIV infection rate twice that of those addicts who did not take part in NEP."

As you can imagine this story and others questioning the value of NEP were widely and loudly discounted and often defamed by the supporters of NEP and InSite. All kinds of competing studies showing wonderful benefits of NEP and InSite were rolled out, very often with the left wing media falling all over themselves in head nodding.

But the most definitive, unbiased study of NEP effectiveness ever done in North America was carried out in Montreal between 1988 and 1995 (see my book *How the granola-crunching, tree-hugging thug huggers are wrecking our country!*, published in 2006). As I point out in that book, a research team led by doctors from the Centre hospitalier de l'Université de Montréal (CHUM), Saint-Luc campus and the McGill University School of Medicine followed 1,599 subjects over a period of seven years.

The results were devastating for the supporters of NEP, or at least they should have been if those on the left paid any attention to legitimate unbiased research.

The Montreal study concluded, "Injection drug users have a higher scroconversion rate (higher rate converting from HIV negative to HIV positive) when taking part in the needle exchange program than those who did not." While the researchers did not necessarily condemn needle exchange programs they did say, "these worrisome findings, however, raise questions as to the effectiveness of these programs as implemented within the context of prevention and care for drug users."

One of the reasons for the Montreal findings may be explained by something written by Dr. Catherine Hankins, a medical epidemiologist with the Montreal Regional Public Health Department, adjunct professor in the Department of Epidemiology and Biostatistics, McGill University, and Associate Director of the McGill AIDS Centre. In an editorial she wrote for the Canadian Medical Association in 1997, Dr. Hankins said: "There is some concern, that, in attracting injection drug users at highest risk to programs in large metropolitan areas may be serving to foster new social networks. Ultimately we cannot rely on these programs alone to stem the HIV tide. They must be integrated with a wide range of additional services that emphasize treatment and rehabilitation over a punitive approach."

Dr. Hankins goes on to say: "In Montreal, needle exchange participants are more likely to have paying sexual partners, to be men who have sex with men and have a higher HIV incidence than non-participants. Needle exchange programs clearly are attracting a higher risk clientele. These findings give rise to concern that large needle exchange programs in metropolitan centres may be bringing together people who otherwise might not meet, thereby creating new social networks and fostering the mixing that has been shown to increase HIV transmission."

It was this report that prompted the United States Congress to refuse to provide federal funds for any needle exchange or similar programs and in recent years the number of locally funded NEPs has been steadily declining as the evidence continues to mount that they only make matters worse.

Despite all of this evidence, however, the promoters of needle exchange programs, in a blatant display of heads not properly screwed on, continue their relentless propaganda campaigns expanding them to include the dispensing of free crack pipes and equipment and so-called safe injection sites.

What is happening in Ottawa is an excellent example of how the propaganda artists have convinced the authorities that terrible failure is really wonderful success. Talk about *Alice in Wonderland*, once again!

Ottawa began its needle exchange program in 1991. A study done by University of Ottawa professor and researcher Dr. Lynne Leonard which was presented to Ottawa City Council, states that in 1992, 10.3 per cent of the injection drug users attending the newly implemented needle exchange program were HIV positive. The same report then goes on to say that eight years later, at the turn of the century, the city's HIV infection rate had shot up to 23 per cent. Four years after that, in 2004, then-Ottawa Medical Officer of Health, Dr. Robert Cushman claimed the HIV infection rate was 21 per cent. Despite the fact that the HIV infection rate had more than doubled during the first 15 years of its existence it was deemed to be such a great success by Ottawa City Council that not only did councillors agree to continue with the NEP, but they decided to start a crack pipe distribution program as well.

It gets even worse. Dr. Leonard's report also states that prior to the launch of the NEP, injection drug users accounted for two per cent of those actually diagnosed with full-blown AIDS. As of 1999—seven years after the NEP started—she reported that figure had skyrocketed to a very troubling 17 per cent.

Similar increases in both HIV positive tests and HIV infections diagnosed have also occurred in Montreal, Toronto and as I have already stated, Vancouver.

In his attempts to persuade Ottawa City Council to launch a crack pipe program, Dr. Cushman was quoted as saying that the capital's HepC infection rate among intravenous drug users was 76 per cent, once again a huge increase from the days prior to the NEP. He stated Ottawa's HIV and HepC rates were second only to Vancouver.

In June of 2011, the Ottawa Public Health department issued a warning that, "The HIV infection rate in the City is the highest recorded in the past decade. From January to April there were 32 new cases reported compared to 70 new infections in all of 2010." Dr. Vera Etches, Associate Medical Officer of Health says the recent increase highlights a need, "To look into what the City can do to protect people from contracting HIV."

And in August 2011 came the shocking news that: "New HIV cases were up by nearly 50 per cent in Ottawa during the first half of this year."

To which I can only respond by saying, "But Doctor, I thought the needle exchange program was introduced to protect people from contracting HIV."

Despite these statistics and many similar ones—their own statistics; their own assertions—the facts which they themselves state, the supporters of needle exchange, crack pipe programs and so-called safe injection sites continue to steadfastly maintain they are very successful. So successful they should be expanded.

If the Supreme Court rules in favor of InSite it is expected that very shortly the pressure will be applied to have the taxpayers fund not only the injection sites, but the drugs as well.

The truly incredible thing about all this is that from day one it has been the left wing that has insisted that drug addicts be supplied with free needles, crack pipe equipment and injection sites, while conservatives have fought for counselling and treatment. Wouldn't THAT be a better form of "harm reduction?" (One of the left's famous bafflegab terms.)

It is disgraceful that in those cities where drug addicts are assisted in their destructive practices there is an almost total lack of assistance of any kind for those men and women who desperately want to kick the habit.

When Ottawa Police Chief Vern White arrived in Ottawa he was astonished to find that residential treatment centres for drug addicts were virtually non-existent. One of the first things Chief White did was launch a six-million-dollar campaign to build facilities for those who want to kick the drug habit and turn their lives around. More than three years later, following incredible heel-dragging and controversy, we finally have a small ten-bed, residential treatment centre for girls.

So even as the City of Ottawa pays to not only distribute thousands of free needles each year, but to pick up more than 700,000 used ones on our streets as well, your chances of getting any help to get off drugs are slim to non-existent. In Ottawa, Montreal, Toronto and Vancouver you will have no problem getting all kinds of help to take drugs. They will even deliver needles and crack pipe equipment to your home. Just pick up the phone and order them like you would a pizza, but God help you if you want assistance to get off drugs because no one else will.

The last time I checked, which was yesterday, not too many chiefs of police in this country are socialists or liberals, (if you know of one please let me know so I can enter the name in the Lowell Green *Book of Astonishing Oddities*) so isn't it interesting that it took a police chief to insist that we help druggies kick the habit rather than make the habit easier for them?

Interesting, too, that it is the Conservative Government of Stephen Harper that is devoting more than $60 million towards a program to discourage drug use and assist in rehabilitation, while the left, which claims to exist on a higher moral plane than the rest of us, continues to insist that it's far better to show the druggies how to shoot up than to help them stop.

I have to ask the question yet again.

Whose head is screwed on straighter? The leftists who say make it easier for addicts to be addicts or conservatives who say let's make it easier for addicts not to be addicts?

I suppose we have to assume that come the next federal election the druggie vote will not go to the Harper Government!

Chapter 32

A Fridge Posting for a Conservative's Kids

Rule #1   Life is not fair—get used to it.

Rule #2   The world doesn't care about your self-esteem. The world expects you to accomplish something before you feel good about yourself.

Rule #3   You will not make $60,000 a year right out of high school. You won't be a vice-president until you pay your dues and earn it.

Rule #4   If you think your teacher is tough, just wait until you get a boss.

Rule #5   Flipping burgers is not beneath your dignity. Your grandparents had a different word for jobs like that. They called it opportunity.

Rule #6   If you mess up, it's not your parents' fault or the government's, so don't whine about your mistakes; learn from them.

Rule #7   Before you were born, your parents weren't as totally out of it and boring as they are now. They will become much more interesting and wiser as you get older.

Rule #8   Your school may have done away with winners and losers, but life has not. Your teacher may give you all the time you want to finish a project and refuse to fail you. This bears no resemblance to anything in real life.

Rule #9   Life is not divided into semesters. You don't get summers off in real life and no employer is interested in helping you find yourself. Find yourself; get comfortable in your own skin on your own time.

Rule #10   Television is not real life. In real life, people actually have to leave the coffee shops and work at real jobs.

Rule #11   Be nice to nerds. Chances are you'll end up working for one.

Rule #12   The empty milk container doesn't go in here!

Chapter 33

English Canada's Culture is
Worth Saving—So Let's Do It!

If there's one thing that drives me crazy on my show it is the assertion by some that Canada has no culture. I hear it all the time. In my previous book, *Mayday! Mayday! Curb immigration. Stop multiculturalism. Or it's the end of the Canada we know!*, I write about an angry caller to my radio show who nearly took my ear off as he boasted that he was sending his son to an Arabic school in Toronto because "Canada doesn't have a culture!"

Actually, when you come right down to it that's essentially what Pierre Trudeau told us in the fall of 1971 when he sprang official multiculturalism on an unsuspecting nation. What Trudeau was saying, although not in as many words, was that while Quebec has a culture worth preserving, the rest of us in English Canada don't have a real culture worth the powder to blow it to hell, so we Liberals are going to give you a whole wagonload of cultures, some of them pretty rotten and primitive, all of which will have equal status.

Quebec, as we all now know, does not consider itself multicultural. In Quebec you are first and foremost a *Québécois* with a culture very well defined and protected by law, convention and custom. No one in Quebec ever suggests the province lacks a culture.

But what about English Canada? And yes, I make no apologies for calling the rest of Canada "English Canada" because that is the language still spoken by the majority outside Quebec, a language that is an integral part of our culture.

So what is English Canadian culture? Does it exist? Can we define it? Exactly what is culture anyway? And to save you the trouble of checking your *Webster's* here's how it defines the word culture: The ideas, customs, civilization, skills, arts, etc. of a given people in a given period.

During a discussion one day on my show concerning the difference between technology and culture, one of my callers hit it right on the head when he said, Lowell, it's easy. Your car is technology, how you use it is culture! It certainly rang a bell with me, because I recall as a teenager piling a bunch of guys into my beaten up old Ford and then driving endlessly up and down the main street of Brantford, looking for girls. Every evening for a couple of years it was the same story and you know something? Our car was only one of dozens doing exactly the same thing and I suspect that's what teens were doing in every small town in Canada at the time. What we would have done if we had actually ever met some girls in our nightly forays I have no idea. It was just part of the culture of the day, just like drive-in movies and A&W carhops. All part of the ever-changing culture of our country.

Whether budding socialists cruised the evening streets of their towns I have no idea. I would assume that rather than drive cars, they all pedaled bikes, but what has become abundantly clear is that conservatives and those on the left have a vastly different view of the Canada of yesterday, today and tomorrow.

To begin with, conservatives know that English Canada is a country with a unique history, culture, institutions and form of government. But most importantly, conservatives know that what has made this country the envy of the world is the commitment of our citizens to a set of fundamental core values. Honesty, self-reliance, perseverance, a work ethic, a belief in God, devotion to family, a sense of fairness, and loyalty to community and country have been and for many of us conservatives, still are at the very heart of what defines Canada.

Conservatives also know, instinctively I suspect, that for any nation to survive as a cohesive national society—and this is especially true of Canada because of mass immigration and multiculturalism—its citizens must be imbued with a strong sense of nationalism and patriotism. Our citizens must understand and honour the unwritten social contract we have created with each other to obey the law, help those who cannot help themselves and maintain strong families and cohesive communities.

Conservatives are also determined to defend our Euro-Judeo-Christian traditions against the onslaught that is taking place in our major cities, our schools and other social institutions. We believe that despite official multiculturalism, our citizens will blend together and live harmoniously only if they are willing, not to discard their heritage, but to recognize that they are first and foremost Canadians. They must realize and appreciate the fact that they are citizens of one of the world's great nations. We conservatives believe that national allegiance and patriotism are the absolute minimum requirements a country must demand of those who enjoy citizenship here. Patriotism—expressed and practiced—is part of the great Canadian culture.

Those on the left, however, don't see Canada in those terms. Far too many of them in fact sneer at some of the values I have just listed, especially patriotism.

"Patriotism," they sniff with disdain, " leads to war." To which I reply, "And thank God for that," because it was patriotism and a sense of national purpose and duty that saved the world, including the socialists, from a fate worse than death during the war with Nazi Germany.

When examined closely you can easily see that the socialists and more than a few liberals tend to view Canada as some kind of work in progress; a grand social experiment that is far removed from the utopia they envisage for us. The concept of core values stands directly in the path they believe we should take. So does patriotism. That is why Pierre Trudeau and his merry band insisted that English Canada's core beliefs and values be diluted, re-shaped—by the importation of the values of dozens of other cultures—all of which according to Canadian law are of equal status.

You would be hard-pressed to find a more drastic social experiment than to purposely erode a successful nation's culture and supplant it with dozens of other far less successful cultures. But that is exactly what the left is up to right now. Look around you! The great social experiment is well under way in Canada.

The left of course is delighted with anything that weakens the Euro-Judeo-Christian foundations of Canada, because whether they fully realize it or not, in their heart of hearts they are filled with self-loathing. They hate the country our ancestors turned over to us. To them allegiance—patriotism—toward Canada is anathema. You don't believe me? Listen carefully to what they are saying and doing.

For the left the trouble started with Columbus. As far as the CBC crowd is concerned Columbus was just another white guy capitalist/exploiter, responsible for a bunch of other white guys stealing this country away from its true owners, the aboriginals. Native Indians, the left steadfastly maintains, lived in the kind of Garden of Eden that they desperately would like to recreate. A perfectly peaceful, environmentally sustainable, socialist community filled with loving families at one with Manitou and nature.

The fact native Indians throughout much of Canada spent most of their time before Columbus, Cartier, Champlain and those other white guys arrived trying to wipe out competing tribes (genocide), had not yet invented the wheel, relied on things like salamander eyes to treat deadly illnesses and made slaves of the enemy's women and children they did not slaughter, is of course just a bit of fiction spread around by white guys like me.

And as for that bit about living in the Stone Age, what a wonderful romantic time it was. The Indians were so concerned about carbon emissions they kept their campfires to a minimum. They ate only berries and the few animals which they very sadly had to kill for their meat and hides. They disdained the use of chemicals, pesticides, nuclear power plants, toilet paper (lack of toilets) and cars and trucks with their nasty emissions. Their villages were all completely sustainable, indeed all their building materials were perfectly compostable and the fact they had no written language meant they could live a far less complicated life than we white guys have forced upon them today. Of course this also meant they didn't have to chop down trees to make paper, which is a good thing—you try chopping down a tree with a stone axe!

And as if the manner in which we stole Indian lands and corrupted them with our white guy ways isn't bad enough, we replaced their utopian lifestyle with capitalism and guys like Mike Harris and George W. Bush, all of which guarantees that in Canada some people, mostly white guys, get rich, while most of the rest of us, especially aboriginals, are forced to live lives of unremitting, grinding poverty, reduced to subsisting on Big Macs, drinking wine from a box and sucking back beer from a can.

Worse, say the lefties, Canada's carbon footprint is unsustainable and we disgraced ourselves by not bankrupting the country by adhering to the Kyoto Accord (a.k.a., the gospel according to Gore/Suzuki).

For these reasons and countless more, the left is certain Canada must be forever changed into a new universal, utopian civilization where everyone is absolutely equal, where carbon emissions no longer exist, all workers are unionized, our military is disbanded except for a small group to fight forest fires and floods, everyone's thermostat is turned down to 14°C during winter and air conditioning is banned in summer. If it was good enough for our brothers of the forest it is good enough for white guys.

Only women will be allowed bows and arrows! Only Gore/Suzuki get a toilet!

And oh yes, I almost forgot; in this sustainable paradise that Bob Rae, Elizabeth May and company will create for us, we will finally get rid of God, Sun Media, Lowell Green, Ezra Levant and Stephen Harper, but keep mass immigration, multiculturalism, humanism, feminism, environmentalism, racial quotas in hiring, gender quotas in hiring, the CBC, political correctness, a separate law for aboriginals, special rights based on sexual behaviour, sensitivity, grief counselling, fairness for all (especially the socialist leaders), and most importantly, equality, not of opportunity but of outcome.

Anyone who chooses not to work will receive a salary exactly equal to that of the prime minister and the head of Shell Oil. We will have heated debates as to whether a duly elected government should be replaced by a series of human rights commissioners comprised solely of former CBC employees. There will be serious thought given to the possibility of the CBC replacing the Supreme Court.

To which we conservatives simply reply: "Look, if you guys want to build yourselves a forest village of deer hide and cedar poles; if you want to eschew electricity, modern medicine, martinis, toilet paper, iPods, automobiles and all the trappings of contemporary society, you go right ahead and fill your hat. But very clearly your heads aren't screwed on straight so just leave me out of your hare-brained schemes."

You live your life the way you want to but I'm not turning down my thermostat or turning in my faithful old Chevy for a stone axe.

That's the difference and that's the problem. Socialism and liberalism are religions whose pastors will not rest until we are all in the same pews, worshipping at the same altar and reading from the gospel of Gore/Suzuki. Folks, with the NDP kiddy gang from Quebec waiting in the wings to take over, might I suggest you bone up on your camping skills!

Chapter 34

Genderless Children

There's something else conservatives have no difficulty with. That is being able to tell the difference between boys and girls. Males and females of any age. (Okay, maybe not always with babies without checking under the diaper.)

You may sneer at this and claim it's a sorry kind of skill, but from what we are led to believe, determining gender is something many lefties have great difficulty with.

I wasn't aware of this deficiency until the story hit newspaper front pages about that goofy Toronto couple raising "genderless," unschooled children.

I didn't think too much about it at first. I mean, when you've been doing a radio talk show for more than 50 years you think you've seen, heard and talked to just about every whacko there is. But then all sorts of lefty letters to various editors began cropping up suggesting, among other things, that there's really no difference between boys and girls.

If boys want to play with trucks, and girls stock up on Barbies, it's only because those are the roles society (you and me) have foisted on them. Left to their own inclinations, the lefties insist, there would be no difference; boys would delight in parading about in pink frillies and play with dolls while girls would stomp fiercely around in army boots and build nuclear bombs using Meccano sets.

Some of the left's leading lights came to the defence of this Toronto couple describing them as brave and groundbreaking. The fact the couple had spent time with some leftist Mexican rebels and then underwent some sort of crash course on communism from the Cubans, seemed to be especially praiseworthy with the granola-crunching, tree-hugging, bicycle riding crowd. (As best I can determine baby Storm's mommy and daddy have not as yet visited Dear Leader in North Korea.)

I thought the pack of Toronto socialists/Marxist-Leninist/anarchists who are always howling about saving public education looked a bit silly defending what they call unschooling, but what the heck, you can't expect perfection even from the "progressives."

I must confess, one of the things that does puzzle me a bit about all of this, is that many of those who claim that identifying gender is discriminatory describe themselves as feminists. We should not be labelling people as boys or girls they insist, or women and men. Genderless is the "progressive way to go"! But then in the next breath these same people proudly label themselves feminists.

Wait just a minute here. If you are a feminist does that not mean you subscribe to the theory that the female gender exists and if there are females surely you must agree there are males?

Apparently Canada is filled with left wing loonies who don't know that our gender is determined shortly after conception, when each parent contributes 23 chromosomes to the fertilized eggs. The father's genetic contribution determines the child's sex, in that he provides either an X or a Y chromosome. The process of physical sexual differentiation does not begin until about the sixth week of embryonic development. Prior to that time the XX and XY embryos are anatomically identical, each possessing a set of female and a set of male ducts.

From what I gather there is a growing belief, at least in the Toronto lefty crowd, that the whole reproductive process needs to be readjusted or, as the "progressives" prefer to say, revisited. Things in the womb were fine and dandy for the first six weeks when the embryo had no particular gender—the two duct thing—but after that things just went haywire. But don't worry, be happy, what God, or nature, or biology has screwed up the "progressives" will get straightened around, and along with just about everything else just simply ban gender. Heather Mallick, I understand, is already working on it.

Rare indeed are those creatures that do not require a male and a female to ensure survival of the species, which is a very good thing. Because, let's face it, if these loony birds insist on genderless children then it's only a matter of time until their gene pool just dries up.

Can't happen soon enough.

It's all very confusing except for conservatives who still cling to the apparently old-fashioned notion that society is pretty well made up of males and females, admittedly with a few other assortments tossed in to keep us guessing.

Yup, unlike the lefties, who seem to believe gender differences are a terrible burden on mankind, we conservatives think this man and woman stuff is not a bad idea at all. How about you?

Chapter 35

Brainwashing Our Kids

At ages eight (Samantha) and seven (Peyton) our grandchildren love to plum the Internet for information on whales, snakes, dinosaurs, and everything else that interests them. They print up a few pages, staple them together, make a few notes and then distribute them to neighbouring mailboxes up and down our road. It's the kiddy version of book publishing and so far none of the neighbours have complained about junk mail.

For the first few times it was all childhood innocence and play, but in the late spring of 2011 it began to take on political overtones. Instead of digging up pictures of a T. Rex or brontosaurus, they instead sought out sites claiming that global warming was going to destroy the planet, polar bears were all starving, and sites pointing out the evils of driving a car. Samantha even managed to find a website claiming that we should stop buying "real" Christmas trees.

I tried to explain that polar bears are not starving, and in fact buying live Christmas trees helps to create larger forests, but it was obvious they weren't buying what I was selling. So into about ten rural mailboxes went some of the propaganda that is helping to make very rich people out of cheats, liars, panic junkies and charlatans.

Believe me, the panic industry is huge and very profitable. One of the things you will notice on all websites warning of a starving this, or a disappearing that, just as with sites about gigantic floating plastic islands, is that they all urge you to donate to their cause and woe betide the world if you do not.

Samantha (at the time of writing, in grade four in Quebec), is the most affected. At nine years of age she is already very worried that the planet will soon burn up and most of the really cute animals in the world are suffering terribly. Since none of this misinformation is coming from any family member I used to assume it's being fed to her at school. When I ask about this I only get vague answers but it's pretty clear most of her classmates share the same concerns.

I'm pretty sure she is getting a healthy dose of this left wing panic mongering stuff from her school, but it turns out a good deal of it may be pumping into her brain from children's TV programming. I'm not sure about SpongeBob SquarePants or the Backyardigans, but lo and behold it turns out that Hollywood has been using shows like Sesame Street to cram left wing philosophy into little brains, and some brains not so little.

There's a new book out entitled *Primetime Propaganda: The True Hollywood Story of How the Left Took Over Your TV*. Author Ben Shapiro says "Sesame Street" is just one of many shows that deliberately creates storylines to advance liberal causes.

Shari Rosenfeld, International vice-president of the organization that produces Sesame Street is quoted in the book as admitting that: "We definitely have a social agenda." That agenda is intended not just to entertain but also to push our culture to the left.

Obviously, this even includes convincing Samantha and Peyton (your children and grandchildren as well) that polar bears are starving to death, the earth will soon burn up because we humans are selfish and drive too many fancy cars and cutting down trees for Christmas destroys forests, thus killing all the nice songbirds.

Shapiro bases his book on interviews with some of the biggest names in the TV industry. Marta Kauffman, for example, co-creator of "Friends," is quoted as admitting, "I mean you have a bunch of liberals running the show." She doesn't deny that in the show, the relationship between Ross's ex-wife Carol with her lesbian lover Susan was intended to push acceptance of same-sex relationships.

I suppose we shouldn't be surprised. After all, Bambi doesn't exactly promote hunting.

The problem now, unfortunately, is that when Bambi first came out, TV was just in its infancy and kids weren't bombarded with left wing propaganda every time they turned around.

In fact, when *Bambi* was in its heyday, most of the entertainment available for kids—movies, television, books and radio—had story lines that in today's terms would be classed as conservative. Good always defeated evil. What today we call family values prevailed. We had Roy Rogers, Superman, Batman and Robin, Gene Autry, and John Wayne winning the war single handedly. *The Wizard of Oz, A Tree Grows in Brooklyn* and *It's a Wonderful Life* were typical movies of the day.

Captain America, Captain Marvel, The Green Lantern, Wonder Woman, The Flash, Spiderman and of course Batman and Superman in the comics. No grey areas anywhere there. Good was always good, evil always evil and good always won. The question of right and wrong was never in doubt.

Early television was very much into strong moral and family values—"Leave It to Beaver," "The Waltons," "Mayberry R.F.D.," "My Three Sons," even "Bonanza" where cowboys set the standard for right and wrong—were powerful conveyors of a time when right and wrong actually meant something.

I know, I know, those shows by today's standards seem kind of hokey, a bit unrealistic. You can poke fun at them all you want, but let me ask you this—if you had a choice of neighbours between the Walton family or that gang from "Jersey Shore," or any of those poor lost souls who ooze onto the "Jerry Springer Show," which would you prefer?

The problem is, of course, very few kids are watching "Mayberry R.F.D." or "The Waltons," but scores of them, sadly, watch "Jersey

Shore" where the sex, booze and partying flow as freely as the "F" word and dysfunctional slutism is glorified.

Thankfully, Samantha and Peyton haven't tuned into anything as reprehensible as "Jersey Shore" or "Jerry Springer," but it's only a matter of time until curiosity draws them there.

You may find my views strange and even if you are conservative you may disagree with me on this one, but I'm not as worried about shows like "Jersey Shore" and "Jerry Springer" as I am about what they are doing with children's shows like "Sesame Street."

At least with "Jersey Shore" anyone with half a brain understands it's pure trash and, in truth, as unrealistic as anything we ever saw on "Leave It to Beaver." My grandkids, and I am sure yours too, have been raised well enough to spot garbage and vulgarity a mile away. Anyone, as my grandfather used to say, with some "proper fetchin' up" will have their heads screwed on straight enough not to let anything as obviously sick and disturbed as "Jersey Shore" or "Jerry Springer" do anything other than provide a few laughs.

But on the other hand, having little sponge-like brains sucked into the left wing vortex by such apparently innocent shows as "Sesame Street" I do find disturbing.

So much so that next Christmas I'm taking both Samantha and Peyton to a Christmas Tree farm where the owner has agreed to show them first-hand how for every tree that is cut at least seven other trees must be growing so that each year another crop is ready for harvesting (since it takes between seven and ten years to grow a

Christmas tree to proper height). And of course, every time one tree is cut another a sapling is planted so that seven years later it's ready for our living room. (According to the Christmas Tree Producers Association, 50 million Christmas trees are planted every year in the US with between 30 and 35 million harvested.)

That should set the record straight on the tree business.

Next on my list, for these little rug rats is a dead of winter trip to Nunavut where they will see that, despite what Gore/Suzuki claim, we still have a bit of ice and snow left and there in full view they'll gaze in wonder as small armies of frolicking, fat polar bears chomp down on seals, raid garbage dumps and drive the locals crazy.

I mean, after all, my first responsibility as a conservative and grandparent is to rescue my progeny from the evil clutches of Hollywood and "Sesame Street" and make sure their heads get screwed on straight.

Chapter 36

Kids do Best With a Mom-and-Dad Family

It's the fall of 1970, a haze of marijuana smoke hovers over most of our cities; a car loaded down with five pot-smoking teens has just ploughed into a transport truck, two are dead, another two critically injured and suddenly parents don't find toking up all that funny anymore.

Caller after caller to my show demand that "someone do something" to stop all the pot smoking. One caller suggests that if the government or the police or somebody doesn't clamp down, Canada will soon have the same kind of drug problem they have in New York City.

"Today it's marijuana, tomorrow it will be heroin," warns another.

Somehow the topic of absent fathers crops up.

"There's too much divorce and too few fathers in our homes these days," claims one of my favourite callers from Pembroke.

I agree and for the next half hour or so the conversation centres around how young boys and girls desperately need positive male and female role models. It's a good discussion; a good program.

But unlike most shows of this nature it doesn't end when I switch the microphone off.

"There's a minister or a reverend or something down here who demands to see you," whispers our switchboard operator, "shall I tell him you aren't available?"

For reasons of security, I rarely engage with someone who comes to the station unexpectedly, but this day something prompts me to take the elevator down to the bottom floor where I introduce myself to a man who, in no small way, changes my life.

He holds out a hand that I immediately notice is missing two fingers. "Hi, my name is Norm Johnson, was that all just talk about boys needing a male role model or are you prepared to actually do something about it?"

Norm Johnson, or Reverend Norm as we all soon begin to call him, is nothing if not direct. Very blunt.

What could I say? He has me!

"What do you have in mind?"

"I want to start an Ottawa Branch of Big Brothers and I need some help. How about it?"

And so, Reverend Norm Johnson, (Reverend Norm has long since passed on) and Lowell Green launch Big Brothers of Ottawa and I get an eye-opening crash course on just how important it is to have both mother and father involved in the raising of their children.

When I say crash course, that's exactly what I mean. Our first problem is raising money. Then, we need to hire a well-trained staff able to arrange and supervise the matches between boys who are missing positive male role models in their lives with men who can provide just that. You can imagine the challenges and dangers involved.

In order to raise money, and in particular convince the United Way that Big Brothers is deserving of their support, I have to convince the community of the need for our services. I need facts and lots of them. I start by talking with several other Big Brother organizations in Canada. Then I spend hours going over Statistics Canada facts and figures, and talk with dozens of single mothers and a few fathers. Much of what I learn is very disturbing.

For example, when we are about to launch Ottawa Big Brothers in 1970 we are shocked to learn that in Canada nearly twenty per cent of our children live in mother-only families. In the City of Hamilton a single mother heads more than 25 per cent of all families.

Of children living with their mothers, more than a quarter of them never see their father from one year to the next—or at best very rarely.

To make matters worse, I learn that these children, boys and girls who live with their mother almost always spend their early school years being taught only by a woman. Their exposure to males is minimal.

Even in homes where the father is present, research indicates that the average father spends less than ten minutes a day on a one-on-one relationship with his child. One of the problems, I learn, is that many fathers grew up themselves without a male in their home and have very little understanding of what it means to be a father.

Happily, the percentage of single parent families, after peaking a few years ago, has declined somewhat since Reverend Norm and I founded Big Brothers of Ottawa. People today are waiting longer to have children than they used to. The divorce rate is lower today as well. Single parent families now average fewer than 20 per cent in most major cities. To give you an idea of the situation as it exists today have a look at the most recent figures available from the 2006 census. As you can see, the number of children being raised in single parent households is still heartbreakingly high.

City	Total Families	Single Parent Families	
		Female only	Male only
Calgary	295,345	33,610	8,610
Edmonton	284,400	36,800	9, 285
Montreal	994,960	144,735	35, 490
Ottawa	314,310	41,405	10, 205
Toronto	1,405,845	197,595	39, 835
Vancouver	580,120	71,250	16,870

Today, single parent families comprise, on average, between 16 and 18 per cent of the total number of families. In most cities, women head about 75 per cent of all single families.

The more we research the need for Big Brothers in Ottawa, Reverend Norm and I both become convinced that no matter how wonderful a mother is and how hard she tries—and most of the mothers we talk with try very hard indeed—she cannot replace what a father provides a child, and despite the insistence of many feminists, there is a great deal of scientific research that even today's modern mothers are typically more nurturing, soft, gentle, comforting, protective and emotional than fathers.

The research indicates that fathers, on the other hand, tend to be more challenging, prodding, playful; they encourage risk taking and engage in more physical activity with their children.

I suspect that most of you don't need formal research to prove any of this. That's the way it was when you were growing up and that's probably the way it was and is with your children and grandchildren.

I know that many on the left will claim what I am saying here is stereotyping and perhaps it is, but that doesn't mean that what the research shows isn't true. And I will tell you something else, in our heart of hearts, most of us know what I am saying is absolutely true. There are exceptions, of course, my mother was anything but nurturing, soft and gentle but at least, thank God, I had positive, strong male role models in my uncles and paternal grandfather.

But what happens to those boys who have no positive role model?

Most of course grow up to be fine, upstanding, productive citizens, but sadly crime figures throughout North America all point to one thing:

Those boys who grow up without a positive male role model are much more likely to live dysfunctional lives and end up in jail.

In fact, a paper presented at the Annual Meeting of the American Sociological Association in San Francisco in 1998 stated: "The strongest predictor of whether a person will end up in prison is that they were raised by a single parent."

The relationship between crime and girls raised in a single parent situation does not appear to be as pronounced as with boys, but there is no question that girls, as well as boys, need strong, positive male as well as female role models, which is something Big Sisters strives to provide in a world where an increasing number of fathers now have custody of their children.

There is, for example, a good deal of research and anecdotal evidence that girls rely on their fathers to develop a sense of their own femininity. A girl's relationship with the opposite sex seems to be based on how well she gets along with the first male in her life—her father. A daughter learns from her father that she is worth being loved by a male. If a father has a loving relationship with his daughter, she will have a better chance of creating a good relationship with a male partner later in life. We are all aware of the fact that very often those women who find themselves in an abusive relationship are simply reliving the lives they led as children.

Despite what the feminists and others would have you believe, a strong relationship between a man and a woman gives children of both genders the best chance of living a full, rich, productive, well-adjusted and happy life.

That is not to say that children cannot grow up as healthy human be-ings in other sorts of relationships. In fact the majority of children of single parents do just fine, as do children whose parents are involved in a same-sex relationship, but even the divorce courts today recognize the value of having both parents involved in the raising of children and because of this, in most cases judges are anxious that the father as well as the mother stay involved in the lives of their children.

Despite what the left would have you believe, there are mountains of evidence, including that which I saw with my own eyes as chairman of Big Brothers for several years, which back me up, that show:

Having a mother and father in the home gives the child the best chance of growing up strong, loving, independent and happy. Hav-ing a mother and father in the home gives children the best chance of becoming good parents themselves.

Chapter 37

The Chimney Watchers

One of my late father's most delightful short stories concerned the "chimney watchers" of the tiny community of Arthur in southwestern Ontario.

When he was growing up, almost everyone in the village was a chimney watcher during the cold winter months. It was pretty easy to do. First thing after shaking yourself out of bed in the morning you stoked up your own fire and then checked your neighbour's chimney to make sure smoke was curling up. You paid special attention to the homes of widows or the elderly. No smoke usually spelled trouble. Sickness, a fall or sometimes what they all dreaded—a death.

Nobody thought it was anything special. It was just being neighbourly, something you knew your neighbours would do for you if the circumstances required it.

Please note that during the time my father wrote about there was no 911 system for instant police assistance, in fact few homes in those days even had telephones. If there was a serious illness or accident there wasn't an ambulance you could call, so you recruited a couple of neighbours to help, hitched a team of horses to a sled and did your best to get to a hospital as quickly as possible. The more affluent might have a car, but chances of getting it started when the temperature was well below zero were pretty slim.

It was not an easy life and few among us would choose to return to that kind of existence, but those villages did have something that is so sadly lacking today in our communities. In the modern, "much improved" society in which we now live, there is little time or inclination for neighbours to look out for neighbours.

Today, it's the huge army of government workers who "check chimneys" for smoke. Not literally of course, we pretty much don't allow smoke in chimneys anymore, but you know what I mean. If there's a problem of any magnitude we expect someone from the government to take care of it for us.

Unfortunately, the more we look to government to take care of us, the more it costs us and ever higher do our taxes go.

Heaped atop all the government assistance are a myriad of large institutionalized charities, pleading for every conceivable cause from cancer research to hamburger for food banks. Don't get me wrong, most of these are very worthwhile causes and Canadians are famous for their generosity.

But for many people, in particular older conservatives, there's something missing with so much of this impersonal giving. A complaint I frequently hear goes something like: "Oh I pay into the United Way and things like that and I'm sure it's very worthwhile but it's so impersonal; it just lacks the personal touch."

That's why you'll see the socialists out on the streets, along with the Marxist/Leninist/Communist/anarchists protesting the latest "Harper outrage" while conservatives, and to be honest, more than a few liberals, are quietly volunteering with the Heart and Stroke Foundation, taking an elderly neighbour to her doctor's appointment, coaching Little League baseball or Timbits hockey, because it is the more conservative minded among us who recognize the fact that not only can't government look after all our needs, it should not even try. We don't have smoking chimneys that need watching anymore, but there is still a lot of neighbourly caretaking that needs to be done.

No matter how they vote, for the most part it is conservative-minded people who care enough about their neighbourhood, their community, their city and their country that they are prepared to do something more than just complain or make a yearly donation to the Red Cross.

I am not suggesting that you won't find NDP, Greens or Liberals volunteering their time or helping out a neighbour; many do, but what you've got to understand is that demanding that government take care of us is what defines the left wing. The more you expect government to solve our problems and provide for us, the further left wing you are, so it is only natural that the further right you go, the less you want government involvement in your life.

Those chimney watchers of my father's time may have voted Liberal (they sure as heck didn't vote NDP), but by nature and circumstance they were conservative-minded. The idea that the government would check their neighbour's chimney never entered their minds. In fact, governments at all levels played a minimal role in their lives. A few neighbours got elected to town council, they hired a police chief, bought him a pair of handcuffs, bought a water truck for the volunteer fire brigade, and hired a local man to plow the village streets during winter. The same guy would probably be in charge of shooting any rabid foxes that wandered into town. The council might debate for a few hours but finally agree to give each of the three school teachers a $50-dollar-a-year raise; they collected a few tax dollars from each farm and business and that was about it. I once served on a small town council of this nature where my job was to get a few guys to remove broken-down old cars off the side of the road.

In my father's time, and even when many of us were growing up, the local churches took care of any charitable needs. The Protestants took care of the Protestants, the Catholics, the Catholics. It was, once again, neighbours looking after neighbours.

It is in that spirit of neighbour helping neighbour that makes such a success out of any appeal I may launch on my radio talk show. It's hardly a secret that the great bulk of my audience (far more people listen to "The Lowell Green Show" than to any other radio station during that time period in Ottawa) is conservative-minded. And as true conservatives have always done, when confronted with real need, they roll up their sleeves and do whatever they can to help.

Whether it's money to send the veterans of Ortona back to Italy for an historic Christmas Eve dinner with the Germans against whom they fought, fund a life-saving trip to the Mayo Clinic for a young Ottawa Valley boy, or an email campaign to stop eco taxes, my conservative listeners do what conservative-minded people have always done. They check their neighbour's chimney, see a need and do what their very nature demands—help.

Don't misunderstand. I know there are plenty of mean, miserable beggars out there who may vote Conservative. I am fully aware there are those claiming to be Conservative who would gladly rob you blind and kick you when you're down.

Some well-known Conservatives have even been known to spend time in jail, and more than a few of them should have.

Yes, it is true. I know this will shock and awe you, but not all conservative-minded people are nice and conservatism is far from perfect.

Conservatism is, after all, a little like democracy itself—far from perfect but when you compare it to every other political philosophy that's out there, you've got to admit:

The best chimney watchers in the world are conservatives!

Chapter 38

Clarifying Left Wing Gibberish

Orwell called it "Newspeak." In the world he created in his book *1984*, words took on entirely different meanings than had hitherto been the case. The intent was to make it a "thought crime" to hold any opposing views towards the ruling regime. All "Oldspeak" was to have disappeared by 2050, at which time all words would reinforce the domination of the State and remove any need for independent thought.

As Ezra Levant and more than a few others in Canada have learned, while the word "thought crime" hasn't as yet entered our lexicon, harbouring thoughts our left wing human rights commissions do not approve of can get you in big trouble and cost you a bundle.

But for the most part the leftists use "Newspeak" only to confuse and frustrate those of us knuckle-dragging "nonprogressives."

The fact is, we conservatives think differently than those on the left and thus it is very difficult sometimes for us to fully comprehend the true intent of the esoteric jargon used during the nonsensical blatherings of pseudo scientists, academics, environmentalists, animal rightists, windmillists, solar panelists, save the polar bearists, hug the thugists, G20 and Vancouver riotists, and so on.

As a professional communicator with more than 55 years of experience, please allow me to add some (dare I say it?) "transparency" to the muddy field of political correctness and provide "Oxfordian" definitions for various left wing words, phrases and rants.

Note: Italic text in brackets are my keen observations, which I feel I owe the world.

A—Everybody gets one of these—along with free cornflakes—in our public schools. Presto! Everybody's a big winner. *(No losers with socialism!)*

Al Gore—American winner of the Nobel Peace Prize for Fiction. *(Also multi-millionaire inventor of the Internet; also the telegraph.)*

Archaic—All conservative thought.

Atomic bomb—Racist weapon dropped on a pure and innocent nation by war-mongering Americans.

Academia—Where all conservative thought and speakers are prohibited and rightly so.

AIDS—Terrible disease spread by conservative refusal to provide free condoms and sex education to kindergarten students.

Air conditioning—Cause of three-headed sheep resulting from ozone depletion.

Atheism—The only religion allowed in our public schools. *(Except for a few scattered mosques.)*

Balanced news coverage—Invented and presented exclusively by the CBC. *(Okay, okay, sometimes* The Toronto Star.*)*

Bible—The world's most dangerous book. *(Along with this one!)*

Bicycles—Mode of travel for the morally superior. Best method of saving the planet. *(Wonderful supporter of the Chinese spandex industry.)*

Big Business—Inventors and perpetrators of slavery. *(Not including big unions.)*

Bigot—Anyone who wins an argument with a lefty.

Bill Clinton—Poster boy for safe sex.

Bilingualism—The aspiration of every decent Canadian. Method of keeping Western riff-raff out of Public Service.

Blanding's turtles—Find one of these little bum-breathers and you can bring all development to a grinding halt.

Budget cuts—Always only to vital core services. Only justified when involving the military. Always carried out by Conservatives. *(Liberals and NDP only increase budgets.)*

Bum—Innocent victim of vicious capitalist system. *(See Big Business.)*

Canada—Country filled with idiot Conservative voters.

Canadian dream—All shot to hell by Stephen Harper.

Communists—Totally misunderstood idealists slandered by capitalist exploiters. *(See Big Business.)*

Cops—Entirely redundant in a socialist society where crime becomes totally unnecessary.

Cow—Dangerous emitter of methane gas.

Crime—Created by cops and capitalist exploiters. *(See Big Business.)*

Death—Fate of the planet if we don't send Gore/Suzuki and the Green Party money and install those little twisty light bulbs.

Debauchery—Unique art and lifestyle that must be supported by governments. *(Along with hand dancing.)*

Defence—Entirely unnecessary in a socialist world where all people love and cuddle each other constantly.

Discrimination—Carried out exclusively by whites against visible minorities even when the whites *are* the visible minority. *(Increasingly common.)*

Diversity—White guys bad; everybody else good.

Don Cherry—A national disgrace. Responsible for the Taliban.

Dumb—Quebeckers who voted for any MP over the age of 21.

Earth—See definition of "Death."

Ecology—Next to Islam, the greatest religion in the world today.

Education—Standards must be lowered to ensure no one fails. Place to pour milk over cornflakes. *(Sometimes mistaken for breakfast restaurant.)*

English—Language soon to disappear in Canada. Language of colonist exploiters and destroyers of aboriginal peoples. Half size on Quebec signs.

Entitlement—Every Liberal is entitled to his and hers.

Environment—Something conservatives are determined to destroy with their footprints. Heavily damaged by Alberta oil sands, cows, Australian camels and frequent fliers. *(Except Gore/Suzuki.)*

Equality—Orwell got this one right as well, just as with pigs, some lefties are more equal than others.

Extinction—See "Death." See "English."

Extremist—Anyone who disagrees with a lefty.

F—Something teachers in the dark ages used to mark on dumb or lazy kid's report cards. Failing never happens under socialism.

Family—Under socialism we are all one big. Prehistoric fad responsible for world over-population. Gay marriage preferable. *(Fewer kids!)*

Family planning—Free flavoured condoms, abortion on demand, sex education in junior kindergarten. *(China sets the standard.)*

Feminists—Women who self-appoint to speak for all women. Organizers of slut walks.

Global warming—Will set fire to planet if capitalism is not destroyed. Send more money to Gore/Suzuki to acquire Hudson Bay beachfront property.

God—Along with Canadian history and geography the only thing you can't talk about in our public schools. Also, female superpower.

Government—With Elizabeth May as Prime Minister the answer to all of earth's ills. Always available to help in both languages.

Growth—Always bad except when it's taxed.

Hate—Fuel that fires conservative souls.

Hate Speech—Any speech the lefties don't like. Most calls to "The Lowell Green Show" on CFRA, Ottawa.

Health care—Must be rationed to reduce population and make more room for immigrants. Only socialists allowed to use private hospitals.

Heterosexual—Those of us in a sexual rut. Sexually disadvantaged.

Homophobia—Conservatives who insist on wearing pants in the Gay Pride Parade. Rob Ford.

Idealists—The NDP, Liberals, Elizabeth May, Hugo Chavez, Dear Leader Chairman Mao, Gore/Suzuki.

Inclusion—Applies to everyone except white males.

Intolerance—Practiced exclusively by conservative white males.

Job protection—Just for members of powerful unions. Everyone else, tough beans.

Just society—Available to all except white males whose last name isn't Trudeau.

Keen—All newly elected NDP MPs from Quebec. (See "Dumb.")

Kids—Baby goats. Human offspring whose sheer numbers will soon destroy the planet. *(Send money to Gore/Suzuki.)*

Kinfolk—People who marry each other, thus creating idiot Conservative voters in rural Canada.

Knuckle-draggers—See "Kinfolk."

Landfills—Punishment for failure to use the black box, blue box, green bin and just generally being alive. *(The Carp Mountain is an excellent example.)*

Leaf fans –Alcohol abstainers, polite, kind to little old ladies.

Left—Where the "progressives" assemble. Found glued to the CBC, riding bicycles, giving group hugs, stuffing flowers in rifle barrels, saving polar bears, whales, trees, bugs, Blanding's turtles, spotted owls. Always holidaying in Cuba or North Korea.

Liberal Party—Recipient of a terrible, but temporary, injustice on May 2, 2011.

Lowell Green—See "Knuckle-draggers."

Marriage—Ancient custom practiced mostly by "kinfolk." (See "Kinfolk.")

Marxists—University professors, CBC producers, union leaders, brave G20 protesters.

Mass immigration—Gotta keep those Liberal votes pouring in. Necessary to replace exploiting, racist, sexist, homophobic, European, Judeo-Christian culture with much-improved diverse Arab, African, Asian cultures.

Military—Must be trained to provide group hugs, fight grass fires and fill sandbags. *(Guns hurt people.)*

Morality—Out-of-date concept that often leads to uncomfortable conservative-like feelings of responsibility and even guilt.

Middle class—Must be wiped out by high taxes.

Multiculturalism—Goodbye Caucasians. (See "Mass immigration.")

Needle Exchange Program (NEP)—Guaranteed to wipe out HepC, HIV. *(And bedbugs, plugged sinuses, earwax, and flatulence.)*

News—Only the CBC (Or in a pinch *The Toronto Star*) can be trusted. *(Send money to Gore/Suzuki.)*

Omnificent—Nycole Turmel, Bob Rae, Elizabeth May, all Quebec MPs, Gore/Suzuki.

Ottawa—Location of giant tax vacuum, pouring money into conservative pockets. *(Sucking Central.)* Also, former home of Canada's wisest man, John Ralston Saul.

Peace—Achieved through group hugs and long walks on the beach with your enemies. Guaranteed with socialism.

People—Should all be replaced by animals *(except for CBC listeners)* with a few aboriginals thrown in for good measure.

Personal responsibility—Are you nuts? Criminals are the real victims.

Pluralism—Views held by two or more leftists. *(Chinese and Greek restaurants in the same block.)*

Poverty—Caused by heartless conservative-led big business. The root cause of all crime and nastiness perpetrated by victim/criminals. Remedied only by paying higher taxes and/or sending money to Gore/Suzuki. Outlawed under socialism.

Progressives—See "Omnificent." All those who prefer dumps to high efficiency incineration. Defenders of Blanding's turtles, spotted owls, coyotes, green bins, windmills, solar panels, drug shooting galleries and raccoons.

Quebec—The only province with a language and culture worth saving.

Quotas—Required to exclude white males from the good jobs in government.

Racist—Me, and probably you, if you agree with anything in this book.

Rich—Anyone who can pay their taxes. Must be taxed more.

Right wing—See "Knuckle-draggers."

School—The perfect spot to suck self-reliance out of children and start them along the path to nanny statism.

Socialism—The path to Nirvana.

Spotted owls—Find one of these and you can stop all progress. (See "Blanding's turtle.")

Sustainable—A magic word with no meaning, invented by the left to suck billions of dollars at an unsustainable rate from bewildered taxpayers.

Taxes—Litmus test for wealth. Those who can afford taxes are rich and must be taxed more.

Taxpayer—See "Taxes." (*An endangered species.*)

United States of America—War mongering neighbour, would much prefer Palestine next door.

Victory—Something that will be enjoyed by the NDP in 2015.

War—American method of settling disputes. Excuse to drop atomic bombs on kind and gentle people.

Xenophobe—Anyone who loves his or her country. Anyone who knows all the words to "O Canada." Anyone flying a maple leaf flag. Don Cherry.

Zebras—Like every other animal, fish, bird and insect on earth threatened by human-induced global warming which is absolutely guaranteed to first flood the entire planet then set it on fire by the year 2009. (*Quick send money to Gore/Suzuki*).

So please hurry and read this book before it's too late! (Or simply send money to Gore/Suzuki!)

About the Author

In addition to being Canada's most honoured broadcaster, Lowell Green is one of Canada's bestselling authors. His numerous awards include citations from former Prime Ministers Pierre Trudeau and John Diefenbaker and Prime Minister Stephen Harper. He is the recipient of many awards including the Helen Keller Fellowship Award from Lions International, the coveted Gold Ribbon Award from the Canadian Association of Broadcasters, the Lifetime Achievement Award from the Radio and Television News Directors Association, and a special award from the International Olympic Commission for his broadcasts from the 1976 Montreal Olympic Games. He has a wing at an Ottawa Hospital named in his honour and has had a day named after him in the City of Ottawa. A plaque naming Lowell as a "Community Builder" hangs in Ottawa City Hall.

Lowell is the co-founder of Big Brothers of Ottawa, founder of the Help Santa Claus Toy Parade in Ottawa, founder of the *Ottawa Sunday Herald* newspaper (now the *Ottawa Sun*) and co-founder of the largest chain of travel agencies in Ottawa.

Stories Lowell has uncovered, reported on and or written about have appeared in newspapers and magazines around the world, including *The New York Times*, *The Times* of London, *The Washington Post*, *Maclean's* magazine, *The Globe and Mail* and the *National Post*. One of the stories he uncovered prompted a special Senate Commission investigation in the United States

In addition to his writing, Lowell can be heard hosting "The Lowell Green Show" on CFRA in Ottawa, Canada, each weekday from 10:00 a.m. to noon. For years his radio program has been the top-rated show throughout Eastern Ontario and Western Quebec and one of the top-rated talk shows in North America. Two of his historic broadcasts are preserved in Canada's National Archives.

His most recent book, *Mayday! Mayday! Curb immigration. Stop multiculturalism. Or it's the end of the Canada we know!* Has become an international bestseller with copies sold throughout Europe, the UK and Australia.

Mayday! Mayday! is credited with prompting a wave of public concern and anger over aspects of Canada's immigration and multiculturalism policies. A wave powerful enough to embolden the Harper Government to launch a series of reforms including the publishing of the pictures and descriptions of dozens of men wanted for various immigration offences.

It is also worth noting that since the publication of *Mayday! Mayday!* The governments of Germany, France, Holland and the UK have tightened up immigration rules and either abandoned official multiculturalism or have made it clear that all new immigrants are expected to learn the language of their new country and fully integrate into the mainstream of everyday life.